Loving You Big

ONE FAMILY EMBRACING
THE UNEXPECTED

Leah Witman Moore

ISBN: 978-1-954614-60-4 (Hard Cover)
      978-1-954614-61-1 (Soft Cover)

Moore. Leah.

Edited by: Monika Dziamka
Cover design by: Asha Hossain

Published by Warren Publishing
Charlotte, NC
www.warrenpublishing.net
Printed in the United States

To Jordan,
who learned the word "can" when
the world thought she couldn't.

Praise for Loving You Big

*"An intimate portrait of boundless parental love
and resilience told with humor, wit, and a deep understanding
of our humanity. … You will be transformed by it."*
—Diana Kupershmit, author of Emma's Laugh

*"Loving You Big is a beautiful collection of essays that should become
required reading for any person or organization wanting to engage and
create experiences for young people with disabilities and their families."*
—Alex Sarian, President and CEO of Arts Commons, Canada

*"… a wonderful joining of the medical complexity of cri du chat
[syndrome] and the universal simplicity of a mother who loves her child."*
—Dr. Jennifer Ewen Frank, Chief Medical Officer,
Clinically Integrated Network, Theda Care

"Hi, Mama. Drumroll please. I have a big announcement! I love everybody."

"We love you, too, Jordie. But it's really time for bed. Third grade starts tomorrow."

"Oh yeah, baby. It's a party." She waves to her imaginary YouTube viewers.

"Mommy said it's time for bed. Have a big heart and blow a kiss to the world. Make sure you like and subscribe."

She doesn't care that they wouldn't be able to understand what she is saying. What matters is that I understand every word perfectly.

Table of Contents

PART I
A STORYTELLING FAMILY

*"Look closely at the present you are constructing.
It should look like the future you are dreaming."*
—Alice Walker

Hi!

Please excuse the mess. I am in the middle of grading some papers and figure out how to raise a child with a severe disability. My nine-year-old daughter, Jordan, has cri du chat, a rare genetic syndrome that makes life trickier. Therefore, I hope you don't mind if I fold laundry while we chat. Multitasking is the only way I can get through the day.

Let me introduce you to the rest of the family first. Zac, my husband, is just helping Jordan pick out something to wear for her playdate this afternoon. Downstairs, the cheering you hear is from my five-year-old twins, Austin and Oliver. They are in the middle of building a spiderweb with all of my dental floss. It's fine, but definitely check where you are walking. We are a loving, chaotic crew.

You might know a little about us from my blog, *Loving You Big*. I started it because I needed to write to remember who I was before I became a special needs mom. It was my way to make sense of the struggle. And after all, what overwhelmed mom doesn't want to disclose her hopes and fears with total strangers? Each entry was a snapshot of what life really looked like for my family. I received comments from incredible people around the world telling me that by reading our stories, it helped them with their own.

When I came out from behind the writing—of the blog and the book—I realized these were not just the stories of my kiddos. They were the stories I had to tell if I wanted to help change the narrative about how people with disabilities were seen in society. My kids are growing up in a society where many people still have an antiquated idea about what having a disability means. Many are not even aware they have these opinions until they are confronted by them. I was one of those people. However, with the introduction of sign language, countless laps using a walker, and daily wig-clad dance parties, our family knows there is nothing about Jordan that needs to be fixed. It is the world around her that needs to shift. Therefore, we opened our doors to show you that a diagnosis does not define a family.

So, welcome. We are so happy to have you here.

CHAPTER 1
Redefining Connection

I am done being quiet.

It's not that I didn't talk when I was younger; in fact, I used thousands of words a day. Most of my family did—my poor father rarely got to speak more than five a night. "How was school today, girls?" Then he would sit back as my mom, my sister, and I took over for the rest of the evening.

It was just safer being nonconfrontational. I was happy to redirect and let what was unsaid linger. I floated through my uneventful childhood, getting lost in the stories of other people. Shakespeare. Angelou. Morrison. I preferred to read the words of others who redefined what it meant to have something to say.

I thought words were the best way to make connections with people, so I started to practice them. On paper. In short stories. On the stage. I spent hours playing Word Munchers on the computer so my typing could keep up with my thinking. I was comforted being near words, even if I was just writing love stories about Mickey Mouse.

I knew telling stories was in my future, or at least learning how to help other people unlock theirs. I was always interested in what stories were told and who had the opportunity to tell them. I knew I wanted to teach; it was a medium for storytelling. I also knew I wanted to act.

At eighteen, I decided I could combine these interests to become a sign language teacher. This plan was diverted when I realized my college did not have a sign language program. That information would have been helpful to learn from my high school guidance counselor, but he was too busy telling me that Jewish girls should learn to cook, take their "pretty pills," and not worry so much about a job because the focus should be on finding a husband. And instead of replying with what I really thought (thanks to the class on feminism I was taking), I just ignored his terrible advice, applied to college without knowing the nuances, and accidentally ended up in a great school—without my major.

It wasn't the last time I missed the opportunity to say what I was thinking, but as my responsibilities grew, so did my voice. I did become a teacher, of both English and theater, and spent my days doing exactly what I had hoped to do—helping people use words to communicate. I met with administrators to fight for more inclusive texts to be read. I started clubs to allow students new opportunities to write and perform. I partnered with colleagues to update the curriculum so it was more student-centered. Every decision I made was around empowering people to tell their stories—to speak their truths.

After thirty years of relying on words, teaching them every day, I learned my firstborn might never use them. In fact, my daughter changed my entire life with just three words. *Cri du chat.* In French, it means "cry of the cat." In medical school, it means a genetic disorder caused by a chromosomal deletion. In the doctor's office, it means tests and therapies. But at the kitchen table, it means my daughter. Our Jordan.

When you are told your child may never walk or talk, you need to redefine everything you know about communication. You search for new ways to describe despair. You find experts to help you expand possibilities. You become trained to find words in new places. You unearth that sign language pamphlet from the nineties to access a starting point. And your ways to communicate expand. You find new meaning behind her smiles, her dance moves, and her kisses. You see joy with her pointing and her body language. And you revel in her hand signs for *Mama* and *more*.

As Jordan's communication grows, so does mine. I learn to speak up where I never previously did. I weave through implicit biases to advocate for my child. I fight to understand what ableism is and how to eradicate it. I learn how to use my spoken words to amplify the other ways there are to communicate. And my words form questions: Does she understand us? What will her future look like? Will she grow up in a more tolerant society? Will my words make a difference? The answer is: I don't know.

And for the woman who whispered her words, who was afraid to confront, who was worried she would appear combative if she really spoke … she has found something more powerful. Something that encapsulates pride and fear, strength and temerity, sadness and joy, love and comfort: to be a mother and learn there are ways to listen to your child who might not speak.

And when they create the word for that, let me know.

CHAPTER 2
The Beginning

Love begins with daydreaming. Like all couples falling in love, Zac and I spent hours in this imaginative phase discussing the big (politics, religion, morality) and the nitty-gritty (macaroni and cheese: side dish or main course?). We could never have imagined the responsibilities our relationship would ask of us one day. What young couple does?

I was drawn to him immediately. We had both just moved to New York City to start graduate school and study educational theater. Standing in his T-shirt from Amy's Ice Creams, with his warm smile and head of curls, Zac was both handsome and approachable. This was long before a sculptor in Rome stopped Zac on the street and asked to use his face as a template for a statue, then produced paper and scissors to cut out his silhouette. That sculptor made a good choice; Zac was striking.

He was also interesting. He was in my Tuesday evening class at NYU, Methods and Materials of Qualitative Research. Never had longitudinal data been so alluring. I heard him raving about a play he had just seen, *The True History of the Tragic Life and Triumphant Death of Julia Pastrana, the Ugliest Woman in the World*. I had never heard someone speak about theater with such passion. It didn't matter that he wasn't speaking directly to me; I was convinced—about the play *and* the boy. All I knew about him was he had just moved from Texas, he had shortened the spelling of Zachary at age eight, and he worked in the office of our graduate program. Plus, he liked this play. It was enough of an opening to start a conversation.

I navigated the New York subway system for the first time and arrived triumphantly at the theater. I missed the important detail that there was no lighting in this production, as the play captured the true story of a seemingly grotesque woman with an incredible voice, so we were never to see her. We were never to see anything. I spent two hours clutching my backpack, squinting at the dark stage as if it would help me see. It wasn't exactly my type of show, not enough musical numbers. I just wanted to have something to say to him. It worked.

My ability to know his whereabouts was pure strategy. I mean, everyone needed to stop studying to get a cup of coffee at 11:45 a.m. on Tuesdays; he didn't need to know that I didn't even drink coffee. We would just happen to be in the same Starbucks by Washington Square Park at the same time every week. Our meetings may have been a bit contrived, but our connection was effortless.

By November, our friendship was sealed. He had listened to all my former relationship stories like they were episodes of *Friends*. The one where the boy left me a love note on my car. The one where the boy sang an original song about me to my dad. The one who designed whimsical handmade notes. I clearly had a thing for boys who also liked words. According to my journal (a requirement for every English/theater major born in the eighties), the first time he grabbed my hand to protect me from an oncoming cab, I saw a shooting star. As a result of too many romantic comedies as a child, I took that as a sign. We were inseparable. He didn't run in fear after my declaration-of-love email. Seventeen years together and I will never forget that cringey message: *Truth is, Zac, my days are a little better when I get to see you and I wanted to thank you for that. I hope you have a great evening. Take care.* He was polite in his rejection. He knew he loved me; he just wasn't in love with me. Such manners; it only made me like him more.

Then the story gets a little gray, as all good love stories should. Although we were not dating, we were best friends. So, when he invited me to Texas to meet his family and learn how to eat crawfish, I jumped at the opportunity. My friends and family thought it was a quick trip to heartbreak, but I thought it was the perfect way to spend my twenty-third birthday.

When I had my first moment alone with his mom, I abruptly confessed I was in love with her son, because that's a great way to make a first impression. She smiled a mother's knowing smile, made me some artichoke dip, and told me about her theory that "love is friendship on fire." Once we returned to New York, after days of sharing cannoli in Veniero's in the East Village, snowball fights in Central Park, and late-night study sessions in a shoebox apartment, we found our flame.

We dreamed of a life of art. It would be the backbone of our classrooms, our travels, and the plays we wished to see. We spoke of having children with an overabundance of curly hair like their parents' and taking them with us to see the world before we retired in Vermont. Naturally, we would spend our twilight years working in our own theater, converted from a local barn. I knew my heart was safe in his empathetic hands.

We moved into an apartment in Midtown East. There was a perfect view of the rooftop bar where many twenty-somethings in matching button-down shirts would gather after their long day in finance. We would look out the window and play the inner monologue game, imagining the conversations they were having. I would feel very snuggled on my slip-covered mini couch, in front of my maroon accent wall, grading papers and determining the newest method to organize our tiny closet. (Ice cube trays are the most effective way to store earrings in small spaces.) We spent two years living in our Manhattan shoebox, cooking meatballs in our bedroom slow cooker and romantically washing and drying our one set of dishes together. It took us two hours to pick out this first set of shared dishes. Watching us, my mom commented, "If the way you two talk about dishes is any indication of how you will make decisions in your future, you are in good shape." We had the luxury of time then.

During a lull in a particularly quiet Rosh Hashanah service, my aunt Judy reached across my lap and squeezed my hand.

"I have my grandmother's wedding ring. When you are ready, it is yours."

I giggled, remembering it was just a few years ago that she'd had a vision of a potential boyfriend and proudly handed me the sketch of the face she'd imagined. It was a crisp outline of a head with a jaw, cheeks, and some shaggy hair. There were absolutely no features. It was just a blank head. I'd had hope. Even without a lot of luck in the romance department, I figured I could find someone with a head.

Zac was more than just the face I was looking for to complete the outline. He was the only person I could imagine spending my life with. Even though we had talked about getting married, and I knew my great-grandmother's ring was ready to come out of the vault, I was still surprised when he stopped at a playground, coaxed me out of the car in the pouring rain, dropped to one knee, and asked me to spend the rest of his life with him. Under that playground pergola, a space purposefully selected to revisit with our future family, I agreed to officially become his wife.

We moved to Westchester, New York, to start the next phase of our adult lives. He had just gotten a job to start an educational theater program at a local college and I would continue the commute into the city to teach high school. We would spend our evenings talking about our students while we worked on our new home, a Tudor built in the early thirties. With each corner of the wallpaper we peeled, we prepared for our new life. We hung up photos from our wedding and set up a hammock in the backyard, where we would imagine relaxing one day with our children. We had no way of knowing the word *relax* would never be in our vocabulary again. We were building our foundation, not realizing we were cultivating a space that would ground us as we navigated extraordinary circumstances. This became our home, not defined by a child's diagnosis or a catalog of doctors' names. It was defined by a friendship that, somewhere in the streets of the West Village, had turned to love.

CHAPTER 3
Jelly Bean

I first realized I was pregnant when I craved a piece of salmon for lunch. My refined palate usually preferred a dry chicken sandwich or a chocolate chip cookie, so it was an obvious clue. We decided to wait to officially announce it until I was three months pregnant, but we shared the good news with our immediate family.

We loved this baby from the first moment the doctor confirmed the results. When our Jelly Bean, as we called her, resembled a tadpole and was as big as a peppercorn, she accompanied her nauseated mother on an Alaskan cruise with the maternal side of the family. While my sister Rachel, and brother-in-law, Brian took Zac on a beer tour in Ketchikan, I remained on board with the company of my parents—Mona and Lenny—and the only food I could consume: cheddar puffs.

When Jelly Bean tripled in size the next month and was the size of a pomegranate, we traveled to Texas to visit Zac's dad Phil, and his stepmom Debby. I spent evenings curled on their couch in Dallas, eating delicious barbecue brisket, listening to hysterical stories about child Zachary, and imagining our little Jelly Bean also sneaking into the kitchen to steal some jalapeños or making superhero shields with neighbors. I saw Phil's proud face as he recounted his own parenting wisdom (hint: embarrass your children as much as possible).

From there we traveled in a green pickup truck to Houston to share the news with Zac's mom Jacquie, and his sister Amanda. With their matching bottled platinum hair, holiday vests, and sparkling consignment store rings, you could see their sunshine from miles away. There was always a hint of Jacquie's former beauty pageant-winner days in the way she carried herself and accessorized. They were two peas in a pod and loved nothing in the world more than their Zachary—except their Hawaiian ginger body spray.

The first time I heard about Amanda, Zac and I were leaving class and he got a text that said his sister was engaged.

"Oh, she's always doing that. We think she just likes the rings."

He explained to me that his sister had a cognitive disability, and despite feeling like an outsider growing up, she'd never met a person she didn't talk to. By the time I met her a few months later, that engagement had dissipated, and she had moved on to her new "baby." It was someone she had met in the prison where she and Jacquie both worked as correctional officers; Jacquie was a prison guard on death row and Amanda worked in the tower booth. It was a job that gave both a sense of purpose. We never got a lot of details because Amanda always became more interested in her preferred conversational topics: cell phone plans and pickled okra.

We hadn't yet told Amanda about the baby because we wanted to share the news with her in person. We held up the picture of the sonogram we had brought.

"Amanda, we have a picture to show you."

"Oh, cool. Did I tell you guys about the new phone case I got?"

It was the perfect Amanda reaction.

We returned home from our summer adventures, ready to finish out the first trimester. We had been a bit superstitious to tell others before twelve weeks, but now that Jelly Bean had officially become a plum, we were ready to share the news with our larger circle.

I fell asleep that night as Zac told his mom she was free to announce her new role as grandmother.

The next morning, I strategically chose a dress that might emphasize a growing bump. I floated through the day, teaching Global Literature. Never had spending six hours with fourteen-year-old students seemed so carefree.

I met the proud father-to-be in Midtown for a celebratory dinner with my cousin. Zac had taken the train in after work so we could share our good news. I found his face in the crowd on Thirty-Fourth Street. I recalled my mother telling me she still felt butterflies when she saw my father, even after decades of marriage, and how lucky she was to still feel that way. That was the same future I imagined for my relationship.

"I told everyone the news!" I shouted as I ran into his arms. "My students are so excited for us!"

His phone rang. It was Amanda. No doubt excited to share in the excitement of a baby girl—or a sale on ham.

"Hi, Amanda." He smiled into the phone.

His face changed. It was not the face of an expectant father. He exhaled and his knees gave out as I screamed his name.

"My mom …"

He was on the ground in the middle of a sea of people outside Madison Square Garden. We sat there, on the sidewalk, with his head against my stomach, rocking in grief until our friend came to drive us home.

Jacquie's heart had stopped. She was sixty-two. She had been diagnosed with congenital heart failure a few years before, but a pacemaker had kept her vibrant and doing what she loved: working. That morning she had been participating in a routine exercise training at the prison, as she had done every week for the past few years. She wasn't going to let anything slow her down. That was who she was. Strong.

Zac had spoken to her less than fifteen hours ago. I could imagine her cradling the phone receiver long after they'd hung up, smiling into the night sky. She had probably let her dog, Frodo, out for one last evening run while she stood on the porch of her quiet country house. Amanda was probably asleep inside, the television still on. Jacquie would gently reposition her daughter's blanket, as she'd done every night for the past thirty-five years, because your baby is always your baby. She would put on her black satin nightgown, remove six stuffed animals from her bed, and curl into her turquoise sheets. She would fall asleep to a story by Maeve Binchy, as she had done night after night. When she awoke in the morning, she would curl her hair and leave for work with her fresh lipstick and pressed uniform. When she arrived at work, she would have gushed about the news of her new grandchild to Officer Angie, but she was interrupted by the start of the exercise drill.

She couldn't be dead.

This woman had been invincible. A single mother who'd raised two children, one with special needs. This was the same woman who had survived an attack by one of the offenders at the prison where she worked. This was the same woman who, after defending her own life and receiving over one hundred stitches, was discharged two hours later and found helping an elderly woman outside of the trauma center. This was the woman who would come home, change into her vibrant turquoise sweatshirt, and make a gourmet dinner with Kenny Rogers serenading her. Her heart was far too strong and brave to give out so early in her life. I remember thinking, *This cannot be real.*

Another officer had spent an hour trying to revive her, but it had not been enough.

I held my husband. I would hold him onto the plane to Texas, into the funeral home, and for every day to come. During the service, I sat in the first row, swollen eyes, and swollen heart. Clutching the hands of my sister, who flew out from New Jersey, and my best friend, who flew out from California, I was literally surrounded by love. We listened to Zac celebrate a life of passion, love, and humor. I heard him promise to uphold his mother's legacy for our unborn child. A legacy that would include perseverance, humor, kindness, and an obscene number of pink sequins.

My hands moved to my stomach. I willed the joy I felt for the life I was growing to make room for the excruciating grief that had just moved in.

As an English teacher, you are trained to look for motifs when analyzing literature. In one's own life, they are impossible to see in the moment. If I could have reached that grieving couple, sitting on the couch in front of a droning television and eating soggy takeout leftovers night after night, I would tell them to get used to this pain. When the small bursts of energy occurred, the nursery would be painted and the registry would be compiled. Finding the balance between joy and sorrow would become their life's plight. But sometimes, it's just easier to succumb to the sadness.

Grief lands like a thud at your front door. Ignoring it increases its strength. It drowns out all other voices, leaving only the pounding of your own sorrow. It batters your sleep, suffocates you while you are awake, and if you momentarily stifle it, it may reemerge as guilt, fear, or anger.

Thankfully, while grief is heavy, joy is light and can sneak in through the windows. It is a stealthy, steadfast little thing. It will not be defeated. It flashes in a memory. It appears in the face of a grandchild who looks like the woman she was named after, the grandmother she never met. Joy is stubborn and, with enough fight, will endure. Pull back the curtains to give it some room.

CHAPTER 4
Welcome to the World, Baby Girl

My pageant-wave goodbye to my neighbors should have been my first sign that I was not really in labor. My body was completing everything our preparatory checklist covered: something about a mucus plug and pain. Zac and I grabbed our perfectly curated hospital bag and took the bumpy drive to the hospital (they were in the middle of paving the road). They examined me, took my blood pressure, and sent me home. I was in labor, just not enough.

I spent the next few hours laboring with the company of my blue birthing ball and the television. Zac was attempting to catch the last few moments of rest, it was 1:00 a.m., but I was in no shape for sleeping. I woke Zac up with a less-than-graceful growl: "Okay it has to be time."

I tottered my way into the car and pulled the seat belt over my swollen, post-due date belly.

Twenty-four hours of labor later, a bit of hyperventilation, and a lot of breathing techniques, Jordan Eva Moore made her appearance in the early morning of March 5, 2011—a baby-sized, female version of her father, with the face of her grandmother. She had a healthy cry, but stopped whimpering the first moment Zac held her.

Jordan was a perfect, cooing six-pound beauty. While she was successfully passing her Apgar test, I was writhing in a hospital bed receiving a blood patch. I joined the rare club of women whose epidurals leak, causing an insufferable headache. I elected for a blood patch, which was supposed to decrease the duration of the pain; however, this second puncture to my spinal cord caused severe back spasms and only made the procedure more complicated. I cursed the doctor while I literally bit my tongue and forced my body to endure more pain than a mother who had just delivered a child should have to experience.

The doctors assured me the spinal fluid racing to my brain would eventually subside, but it would only be manageable if I didn't try to lift my head and remained completely flat. This bit of advice turned out to be impossible. I was expected to nurse my newborn and heal my body, but not lift my head off the construction paper sheets. Sure.

Yet Jordan's "unremarkable birth," a term used when nothing medically abnormal occurs during delivery, calmed us as new parents. She briefly choked in the nursery, but the nurses assured us it was nothing out of the ordinary. We were new parents; everything was out of the ordinary.

When it was time for my breastfeeding class, I was picked up by an enthusiastic, ruby-lipped nurse who was going to teach me some tips. With Zac's help, they transferred my pounding, postpartum body into a wheelchair. This proved almost as difficult as pushing out a baby. In order to avoid disrupting the spinal fluid, I had to lean as far as I could to the left so I could rest my head sideways on my hand, but if I leaned too far, the incision from the blood patch would create searing pain throughout my body. Yup, perfect shape to learn how to nurse a baby. The nurse carefully pushed me into a small room with just me, a microwave, and a large prosthetic breast puppet named Bessie. I was too exhausted to even ask why we had to move if I was the only student in the class.

The nurse spoke at a deafening volume and demonstrated how to successfully produce colostrum for the baby. Bessie would aggressively approach my horizontally positioned body as if it were a newborn baby. It was all I could do not to shout, "Not a good time, Bessie!" as the gigantic mammary gland zoomed toward my face. Zac probably spent that hour teaching Jordan about the history of the Dallas Cowboys, as is required for every new Texan father. It was the only time in our marriage I was envious I was not receiving a lesson in football.

Bessie, the ruby-lipped nurse, and I wheeled back to the room to find Jordan's new pediatrician standing at the foot of the bed. She waited patiently for me to curl back into a fetal position as she gently explained that Jordan, while thriving, needed surgery for what was considered a "routine procedure." Her anal opening was a bit too close to her vaginal opening and it needed to be corrected. They would schedule the surgery within the week. My heavy head, already in position to catch my pain, attempted to absorb the news, but it just weighed further down on my chest. Was there an intake form where we could check, "No, thanks, routine procedure, we'd prefer to spend time organizing photos of our baby in her newborn outfit like everyone else"? Instead, we scheduled a tour of the surgical wing for the following day.

We have since learned that this birth defect had nothing to do with her later diagnosis of cri du chat. Perhaps it was just a practice round to prepare for the challenging days to come. We didn't want the practice. We were prepared: color-coded, closet-labeled, crib-assembled prepared. Preparation was our anecdote for mourning Jacquie. We had completed parenting class, studied baby books, and stolen a few more pairs of hospital socks than needed. None of those arrangements, however, included how to handle putting your week-old baby under anesthesia.

But first we took her home. While I waited for Zac to return with the car, I snuggled a tiny Jordan and politely listened to the receptionists tell me babies often look like their fathers, because in the animal kingdom it was how they avoided being eaten. As we drove the prerequisite 1.4 miles per hour home with our tiny human, it looked as if the moon were smiling. The photo of a sleeping Jordan in her car seat became the first page of her baby book. Well, the only page. Nine years later, completing the rest of it is next on my to-do list.

We could not wait to introduce her to her perfectly curated room. Joy—a whimsical owl with giant cartoon eyes plastered on a pink body with elongated, orange feet—was waiting in Jordan's crib. A handwritten "I love you" placed in the center of a Raggedy Ann and Andy print, recovered from Jacquie's house, added a touch of sentimentality the baby books encouraged. I'd hung it next to the crib, not directly over it, so it wouldn't crash and fall on her developing eyelids. I was going to be a great mother.

We had one day until her procedure. I spent the evening lying sideways on a couch with an open baby book on the floor, trying to figure out how to nurse. I blamed the searing pain in my head for my inability to get her to latch on correctly. Jordan had spent the evening rooting on Zac's chest in search of milk. It shouldn't have been so hard. Yet I looked like I was trying to build an IKEA futon rather than nourish a tiny baby. I should have paid more attention to Bessie.

I hummed a lullaby from our family songbook, which seemed to calm both of us. I felt the generations of women in our family wrapping their hands around ours. A legacy of tough women. This new little one would fit right in.

The next morning, we packed for her trip to the hospital: diapers, onesies, chocolate bar, extra fluid in my head, fear. All the things you need to escort your newborn baby back to the hospital. At least there was complimentary valet parking. We took a video of her little dolphin noises and tried to soothe her hungry belly with a pacifier, as she needed to fast for the procedure. That just felt like an extra-cruel detail, since I had finally gotten her to latch just an hour before. My father-in-law, Phil, had flown in from Dallas just to hold our hands, and the support allowed us to keep moving forward. A simple "I'm here" goes a long way. When the surgeon came out to meet us, she cradled her arms to take Jordan.

I would not let go.

This was my newborn baby. I had become accustomed to her constant presence for the past nine months. She was too tiny to have surgery. What if she were allergic to anesthesia? What if her lungs weren't developed enough? What if she didn't wake up? It was one thing to rest my recovering body from the physical pain it was feeling, but the emotional pain rendered me powerless.

I would not move.

Zac put his hand on my back. "Leah," he whispered. "It's okay."

A well-kept secret of relationships: you cannot both collapse at the same time.

I trusted his strength. He carefully lifted Jordan from my arms and lovingly transferred her to our understanding surgeon.

A waiting room of anxious parents magnifies every nail-picker, gum-chewer, and coffee-swallower. It was as if there were a megaphone attached to everyone amplifying their idiosyncrasies. I could barely tolerate these sounds on a beach vacation, let alone here. I needed to move. My father-in-law obliged. He made two purchases inside the gift shop: a tiny onesie that read "I Nap Like My Grandpa," and a brownie of the same size for me. I allowed the small café table to take the weight of my head while we waited and I chewed in silence.

When our pager sounded, I was startled by how slowly I responded. Every second of the past ninety minutes had been torture, yet when faced with an opportunity to soothe my child in recovery, I didn't move. I'd already spent hours nursing her and practicing cutting her fingernails, but I had a lingering fear. What if I walked into the recovery room and didn't recognize her? What if we hadn't spent long enough together for her face to be imprinted in my heart yet? What if I didn't know my own child? What if I couldn't handle what I saw?

Seeing her was both dread and dream. Zac grabbed my hand and we listened to the doctor's report. "Successful, a routine procedure." I absorbed the vision of her vulnerable body attached to a battery of wires. The weight of that moment remained with me long after the surgery. She was so fragile, innocent, and entirely our responsibility to keep alive.

When we checked into the hospital to stay overnight, we were in a corner room next to a boy with a broken arm. While there seemed to be a party in his room, we were watching our newborn turn blue because her oxygen levels had dropped so quickly. When we paged the nurse, she sauntered in and checked Jordan's levels with an abrupt and condescending manner. Her response implied that we were being overly dramatic parents and that Jordan was fine. She told us just to keep an eye on her oxygen machine, all night and then strolled out. I remained awake for the entire night, aware of the unnerving beeps of her oxygen machine and wishing I could breathe for her. As the ache from the spinal fluid finally dissipated, the pressure of parenthood took over. I texted my friend: *I'm not sure I am going to make it through the night.* Her frantic response worrying about Jordan's safety was my first lesson in motherhood texting. I could become hysterical and hyperbolic, but I had to be clear that no one was literally dying. It wasn't always a given.

Zac was able to secure some sleep, curled up next to Jordan's hospital crib. I noticed she slept in the same position he did. They still do this. Standing over them, I took one deep breath that was all my own. Perhaps the first I had taken in nine months. *Exhale.* The worst is behind us. *Inhale.* I am a mother.

I am forever learning what that means, not as some picture-perfect mother but a real, sorrowful, and sanguine mother.

With the next sunrise, it was time to bring her home.

Joy was waiting for her.

CHAPTER 5
The Danger of Comparison

I have never been competitive.

When I was in middle school, I would steal the soccer ball away from my opponent and then stop the play to make sure she was all right. I voted against myself in school elections because I really liked the other candidate. I always liked playing games, but I never cared who won.

When one becomes a parent, regardless of circumstance, age, socioeconomic status, or parenting philosophies, we accidentally start to play the comparison game.

"My son rolled over at three months." "My daughter took her first steps at ten months." "My little one recited all of *King Lear* before his first birthday."

It was as if there were a tacit agreement that the child with the Harvard book covers in kindergarten would be more successful. From the moment we received our first score on the Apgar, we prepared for the standardized tests of our future. It's human nature to want the best for your child; it's also acceptable to be afraid of what the alternative means. It was a good thing I didn't seek competition, because the child comparison game was one I would have clearly lost.

As a teacher, I find there are a few buzzwords that get thrown around a lot. "Pedagogy." "Scaffolding." "Differentiation." The ones that assured you an "A" in college: Lev Vygotsky's zone of proximal development. In short, these terms mean children follow their own trajectory toward learning; comparison was not a helpful tool in the classroom. Because Zac and I knew each person developed independently, we weren't worried about comparing Jordan's milestones. She was her own person and would learn when she was ready.

Our little one was struggling with some ear infections, reflux, and sleep issues, but she remained a giggle ball. We were happy she was so happy. The surgery at birth seemed to be just a blip. By four months old, she had perfected what we lovingly called the "giggle and roll." While we knew she was supposed to demonstrate interest in sitting up, and we had been using techniques the pediatrician suggested, she seemed far more content rolling her chubby thighs across the living room floor to find something shiny. She was delightful. She was fine.

Fine.

At six months, Zac joked that at the least she could be a model for steak restaurants. She was blessed with Jacquie's cheekbones and some early-developed sharp teeth, yet preferred to lounge on the carpet rather than do anything else. It was a perfect career option. Put a plate of steak in front of her and let her chew on it for some adorable advertisement. This running joke avoided the larger issue. She could not sit up at six months old, then eight. Humor was a perfectly valid denial strategy. In the security of our home, it was easy to deflect her lack of development. She was fine.

Then day care called. They didn't know how to engage her because she would only lie on her back and smile at the ceiling. They were concerned. I didn't want them to worry about us, because it would force me to consider why they were worried. I brushed it off and said what I thought I should say, something polite and vague. When Zac came home from work, I broached the subject with one more tiresome joke. Jordan was in her first committed relationship with the ceiling fan. It was our last deflection using humor, and we needed to acknowledge the facts. Our child was not developing. It was time to take some action.

I picked up some of my school textbooks from the donate pile that I had never donated. With a flushed face, I read through works I had only studied theoretically, zooming past terms like "atypical" and "worrisome." These references couldn't be explaining our child. We had already gotten through our traumatic parenting moment; surgery during the first week of life should have at least cleared us for stress until the prom.

It was time for some more information. We received a range of responses and extensive co-pays.

The pediatrician was proactive. "Let's start the Early Intervention evaluations and a series of exams to rule out anything too serious."

The audiologist was infuriating. "At nine months, it is significant that she has had sixteen ear infections. Let's check her hearing. Jordan, raise your hand when you hear the monkey clap. No, Mom, don't turn your head when you hear it; that is what we call leading the witness. Inconclusive results."

The ENT was archaic. "You're breastfeeding for too long and it's impacting her milestones. Stop nursing."

The allergist was pragmatic. "Do you live in a high-pollen area? Perhaps she had a bad reaction to the anesthesia at birth?"

The childhood developmental expert was alarming. "This child isn't doing anything. You need to quit your job and transform your home to give her a fighting chance. I don't see a lot of hope."

We returned to our captain, our pediatrician, with the test results. She was concerned. "We are dealing with global developmental delays. Her head circumference suggests microcephaly, an abnormally small head that impedes brain development. I am not sure if her brain is growing. It's time to see a developmental pediatrician."

Then the comparison game changed.

"My cousin's sister didn't talk until she was four, and she's a doctor now." "My neighbor's son's mailman didn't walk until he was three, and now he runs marathons."

When I was a little girl, my father coached my soccer team. I wasn't exceptional, and I mostly did it for the orange slices at halftime, but my father believed in me. He would run up and down the sidelines in his bright red shorts, cheering for me to steal the ball, dribble down the field, or score a goal. His voice would carry, and I would be motivated to stop singing show tunes for a moment and try to play. At least I was a little better than my teammate, who simply sat down on the field and made a bouquet of daisies. I'm not sure we had a winning record that year.

My father used his soccer-coaching voice the day we visited the developmental pediatrician's office. Zac and I had asked my parents to join us; when you are processing challenging information, it's helpful to have more ears. We were welcomed into the room, where we placed an eleven-month-old Jordan on the colorful carpet squares in the middle of the floor. Giggle and roll. Giggle and roll. She was full of glee, even without her beloved ceiling fan present.

The doctor's barrage of questions started. "Does she look at you when you call her name? Does she know where her nose is? Does she pull to stand? Does she tell you when she is hungry?" He placed a pencil on the floor. "Let's see what she can do."

My father started his run down the sidelines. This time he wasn't cheering for his youngest daughter but for his first grandchild. "Jordan, you can do it," he coaxed. "Pick up the pencil. Pick it up, Jordan. You can do this! Go ahead."

Jordan giggled at him and remained completely still.

"Do it, Jordan. You can do it. Pick up the pencil. Pick it up."

"Dad, it's okay. She isn't ready for that skill yet. It's okay."

"She's got this. Here, Jordan, watch me. Pick up the pencil. Pick it up like this."

The doctor made a mark in his notebook.

One hour of this torture. One hour of my father's cheering, Jordan's giggling, and the doctor's notations. She did not complete even one of the prompts the doctor instructed. He should have asked if she could laugh; she would have aced that. The desperation in my father's voice was more than I could handle. I wanted to get out of there. If there was something wrong with my daughter, it meant there was something wrong with his grandchild. We were a family that found solutions, but I couldn't run faster down the field, practice my dribbling, or shoot higher to help Jordan pick up that pencil.

I have since learned it's a common sentiment that a child with special needs can be fixed. Many families of special needs children desperately try to love the disability out of them. We did everything right during pregnancy. *If we spend more money, visit the right doctors, or eat something like ginger-soaked marzipan, we can make it go away.* Sometimes you just can't. We must sit in the discomfort of not knowing. That is the hardest part of the entire journey, breathing in the uncomfortable and letting it linger.

I felt hopeless; I could not duplicate for her what she was supposed to do independently. And I was afraid. When you look at your child as if in slow motion and realize there is something wrong … when there is not enough will, bargaining, or coaxing that can change your situation, grief moves back in.

One week later, we received the paperwork from the developmental pediatrician. Jordan's results concluded that, at eleven months, she was meeting the milestones of a newborn. Less than 1 percent on the scale. "We don't often like to say 'zero,'" the receptionist added. "I'll get you a referral for a geneticist."

I have very few pictures during this time. In fact, I avoided most photo opportunities. I didn't want a photo from Easter with Jordan in a highchair while her younger neighbors were toddling around in front of her. I didn't want to remember another barbecue where she lay outside on a blanket, staring at the trees, while babies were crawling over her. Some days I would lie to my coworkers ("Yes, she is about to walk any day now.") Some days I would redirect the question ("Oh, nothing eventful here. How was your ski trip?"). An anecdote about Bessie, the prosthetic breast, was a great distraction. Most days I would just smile and comment on the challenging adjustment to parenthood ("You know, busy, busy").

Despite all the data, we hoped this phase was just a minor setback, an aberration. A moment to celebrate during all her milestones: bat mitzvah, graduation, wedding. "Our little steak model was a late bloomer, but let's celebrate her now with a nice prime rib." *Chuckle. Chuckle. Glasses clink.* If you really zoomed in on any photograph from that time, though, you would see us, forced smiles, tired eyes, and complete desperation in our hearts. Fear does that to you.

CHAPTER 6
Happy Birthday

"Would you excuse me for a moment?" I whispered, sneaking past the guests. "I just have to grab something from upstairs."

The theme was polka dots. Our closest family and friends congregated around the Pinterest-inspired room. Assorted colors of paper plates were affixed to the ceiling, streamers artfully strewn, creating a whimsical setting. I had agonized over her perfectly constructed smash cake. We were ready to blow out the candles.

Except I was upstairs, in my closet, crying uncontrollably. Alone.

We were up to our eighth specialist in three states. We were awaiting blood work from the geneticist's office. We were no closer to an answer.

This was her first birthday party, and we had over thirty guests waiting downstairs to celebrate her. I had only one thought: *This day is a celebration of everything she can't do.*

"I'll be right down. I just need to grab more candles," I lied from the top of the stairs.

I huddled in a ball on the floor of my tiny closet that was barely large enough to hold all my stained, oversized sweatshirts. It felt like the right setting for a mother with a theater background in the throes of a breakdown. I had done everything a mother was supposed to do.

Just 365 days ago, Jordan had come into the world. I had whispered the words to "Happy Birthday" as she purred in her sleep. "Welcome to the world, baby girl. We are going to make an incredible life for you." She was received by a loving family and an Italian aria from her uncle. Her entrance was also marked by an excessive number of photos, even if some of them had oxygen tubes in them.

I had learned to nurse. I had learned how to administer her reflux medicine without staining her onesies. I had learned to toss her in the air to make her laugh. But while my friends continued to turn the pages in the prerequisite handbook, I was floundering. By her first birthday, I had hoped that all the things we were waiting for would just magically occur.

When I was preparing the food before the party, I burst into tears because I couldn't figure out how many pizzas we needed. My brother-in-law calmly helped me work through the simple numbers, and when I turned to him, embarrassed about my uncharacteristic outburst, I whispered, "This isn't about the pizza."

"I know," he said and lovingly squeezed my hand.

I swallowed up whatever it was that had begun to leak out, as if I were taking a shot of some potent alcohol, and continued to move through the party prep. I couldn't have known it then, but I had repressed my anger so much that when emotions did arise, I thought it was sadness. But this was not sorrow. This was Charybdis, whirling in the pit of my stomach. (Because when English teachers have emotional breakdowns, only ancient Greek mythology will do.) Of course, we were sad she was struggling, but I was furious about what had become our normal. This was not supposed to be our story. Zac and I had worked hard for a beautiful life together and we deserved to be blowing out the candles on our daughter's cake without any doubts in our mind.

But anger had not been a frequent visitor in my life, so I didn't know where to begin to release it, or how. So I let it simmer as sadness. Sadness was much easier to cover up with a fabricated smile, even if the guests downstairs were not convinced. No one was going to throw me off my tower, even if they could all see it teetering.

I knew there would be small talk and chatter until I returned. I knew Jordan would be there, in the center of the room, banging on the tray of her decorated high chair. I knew she would be sitting in front of twelve photos, one for each month of her life. Despite the constant sickness, testing, and prodding, she was beaming in every photo. Missing this milestone was not an option.

I splashed some water on my face and then walked down the stairs. With a deep breath, I grabbed the smash cake and found my husband's brave face in the crowd. "Polka-dot socks," he said with a wink. "Good touch."

Reason #7,042 why I love my husband. He was just as nervous, overwhelmed, and terrified, and maybe even as livid as I was, but that twinkle in his eye always grounded me.

We took our positions, proud parents standing on either side of the decorated high chair. The rendition of "Happy Birthday," in harmony, was especially beautiful as a result of the talented actors we were friends with. We were worried about Jordan's quality of life, what the year to come would bring, but as we stood there, encircling her with our devotion and an unwavering support system, we blew out her candles. She looked up at us as if asking permission, then directly face-planted into the lopsided, yellowy goodness. Pulling her head back, she looked alarmed, and as a clump fell from her eyebrow onto her belly, she did what she does best: giggled. Even then, it was her small signal about how she would approach the world.

CHAPTER 7
Priorities

I was the last person to see my grandfather before he passed away. Zac, Jordan, and I drove to New Jersey to see my Grandpa Sy, who was now in hospice. We had grown accustomed to walking through the door and hearing his booming laugh and the *ba-dum-bum* of his favorite joke, so this time, the quiet of the house was deafening.

Zac remained with a sleeping Jordan, while I went up the stairs to sit with my grandpa in his room of the past sixty years. He was frail, but he smiled when he heard my voice. He motioned toward the window and asked me to move the curtain aside to "make more room." He then started talking to someone else in the room. He talked about dinner and a shirt he was going to wear to a meeting. I didn't ask, but I knew he was talking to my grandmother, a woman I had never met. I was no longer a granddaughter worrying about my grandfather. I was a spectator in a life lived long before me.

My grandpa's gaze rested on his front yard, and we were back in the 1950s, where my dad and uncles would play ball outside the house. Well, at least the three older ones would play while the youngest was used as the base. My grandmother had tried her best to discipline them. She used a chalkboard to record their daily misbehaviors and would sternly tell them, "Wait until your father gets home." But the boys had perfected their system of distracting her while another one erased the board, so when my grandfather returned home, he would only see an empty slate and a tired wife who couldn't remember the infractions. He had worked two jobs so he could provide a better future for his family. He was a patriarchal pillar of my family, and for a brief moment, I didn't just hear the stories; I watched him live through them. I sat by his bed and listened to him talk to my grandmother, his Bubbe. When he dozed off, I kissed him, told him I loved him, and left. He died the next day.

There are a million stories I have about my grandfather, and in each one, I can remember a lesson he wanted me to learn. When he came back from World War II, he went to school on the G.I. Bill and got a graduate degree at Columbia University, but he couldn't afford to rent the cap and gown. So, with his loving Bubbe and children by his side, he proudly watched in the stands from afar, as the first member of his family to receive a higher education. He valued education, and he passed that value on to my dad and my uncles. He knew what it meant to work hard. While I know the final moments of a person's life may never quite be what they seem, the last conversation he may have had was about dinner and a work shirt. It could have been his illness, but I like to think it was his last lesson: enjoy the simplicity of life. Be with the one you love, surrounded by your family.

After his funeral, I continued to balance parenting a child with delays, working a full-time job, and completing the work of my doctoral program, studying English education at his alma mater. But no matter how fast I moved, there were still too many decisions that needed to be made in a fixed period, and I was becoming overwhelmed by all the choices. Decision fatigue, as the caretakers of the world call it. I was currently spending a large portion of my time on my pre-dissertation research, the dynamics of play in a secondary English classroom. Zac and I had created a color-coded plan about how our schedules could accommodate the extra hours and therapies Jordan needed. However, when it came time to focus on my school assignments for my doctoral program, I found myself staring at a blinking cursor. It was the first time in my life I could not find words. I was tired, but not the kind that sleep would fix. I needed a break. Zac and I discussed that it wasn't just time to rearrange our calendars, but also the priorities of our lives.

I withdrew from the program. I have never regretted my decision. One can never regret putting what matters first.

CHAPTER 8
On the Day of Our Diagnosis

College acceptance and rejection letters come in two very different envelopes, a small one with a "no, thank you" letter or a large one with the welcome packet information. The phone message from the geneticist's office was the equivalent to the welcome packet: "Mr. and Mrs. Moore. The results are ready."

Since Jordan's inception, we had been learning to live an unexpected life. I announced becoming a mother twenty-four hours before my husband lost his. We spent the first year as parents carrying a medical binder that weighed more than she did. We kept moving forward. We gained tools to manage our expectations. We thought that would be enough to prepare us for the answer to the lingering question, what was going on with our child?

Sitting in the corner office, moving the wooden balls back and forth on the worn-out busy cube that is a prerequisite for every doctor's office, we awaited the results. Jordan bounced between us, preoccupied with the glasses on my face. We thought we had prepared ourselves for the news we were about to receive. Perhaps an answer would create a plan of action, a break from the year of doctors, but no preparation is possible for life-altering news. The geneticist's tone was filled with a mixture of pragmatism and compassion. This wasn't her first time stating a diagnosis—she was a professional.

When she uttered the phrase "cri du chat," it was like my body immediately knew what it was, even though I had never heard it before. She briefly explained key facts. Jordan was missing part of her fifth chromosome. Cri du chat had been discovered by a French geneticist, Jérôme Lejeune, in 1963. It is quite rare, occurring in one in 50,000 births, most of which are caused by spontaneous deletion. However, our case could be genetic, we were told, so the entire family should receive more testing. The syndrome resulted in substantial developmental delays and most of the children were not expected to walk or talk. I held my breath, as if trying to memorize information for a test I had forgotten to study for, clutching Zac's and Jordan's hands. These words would redefine us all.

I thanked the geneticist for the data. I was overly polite. Awkward, in fact. Zac clarified information from the past year that now made sense. Jordan's choking in the hospital, her constant ear infections, and her eye gaze were all characteristics of the condition. Her little dolphin voice was referred to as a catlike cry, the English translation of the French term *cri du chat*. That is why a stranger at the airport had thought I had a kitten in my baby carrier and not a six-month-old child. They were all markers we didn't know we were supposed to be looking for.

The geneticist advised us not to over-research the condition but to rely on the cri du chat community, the 5p- Society. The web page showed a child who looked exactly like Jordan. The geneticist suggested genetic counseling before we considered having more children, and encouraged us to focus on our marriage, as the rate of divorce can escalate with additional stress. Then things get a little hazy for me.

Memory is imperfect, especially in a heightened state of stress. Perhaps Zac and I hugged, or maybe we just paid our twenty-five-dollar co-pay and made another appointment. Perhaps one of us said something wise, or maybe we just talked about takeout. There is only one fact I remember: Jordan's laughter.

I could not safely drive all the way home through my blurred tears. I pulled into the parking lot of the local bank and turned off the engine. I closed my eyes, trying to actively swallow the sorrow I felt brewing in my stomach. In trying to block its path, I released a guttural noise that caused Jordan to giggle. The shock, the stress ... my mind was in turmoil—but I looked in the rearview mirror and saw a smiling Jordan. She was the same, even though I had just changed significantly. It was enough to get me to turn the car back on.

During the remaining five minutes of our drive home, she waved at me through her car seat mirror. I had gotten used to her silence while we were driving, but one day it might be a fifteen-year-old version of her, just waving.

I couldn't do this.

I had told myself that any information would be helpful. To know what was causing her severe delays would mean I would know how to help her. But, I was wrong. *Why is this happening? Can we keep her safe? How are we going to tell our families? Can our marriage handle this stress? Should we have more children? Will she live a long, healthy life?*

I didn't know what to do first, but my base instincts knew I needed to get her to food and safety. I stumbled through the door and created a nestled spot in front of *Mickey Mouse Clubhouse.*

I was not strong enough for this.

Will she have friends? How will we potty train her? Can she be potty trained? Will we have to physically carry her for the rest of her life? Do we have to make our house wheelchair accessible? Should we learn sign language? Can she have a bat mitzvah? Should we move? Will she have behavioral problems? Can we afford her medical bills and therapies? Will this change how happy she is?

I don't know which of these questions I said aloud to Zac or if I said any of them at all. I replayed the life I had imagined for her: walking her to the bus stop, driving her to college, watching her walk down the aisle and move into her first home. While she watched Mickey and his friends do the "Hot Dog Dance," I was rewriting an entire life that I had imagined for her.

Food. My world was crumbling; I couldn't also marinate chicken breast. By some cosmic miracle, my incredible college roommate was visiting from Los Angeles. She knocked on our front door and dropped off Chinese takeout just in time to catch me.

"I love you," she said, guiding me into the kitchen. "I'm here. Let's start by eating." She scooped up Jordan and swung her around, just as she had on every prior visit.

"What will we tell people, Zac?" I mumbled.

"The truth."

I had never been great with the truth. It wasn't so much that I lied; I just often said what I should rather than what I wanted. Call it what you will: nonconfrontational, overprotective, avoidance-prone. We sat down, called our families, and then composed the following email for our extended network.

> *November 26, 2012*
>
> *We finally got a diagnosis.*
>
> *Of course, this information is hard for us to process. In short, we were told we are raising a child with significant cognitive and physical needs; however, we were also assured that with follow-through, continued Early Intervention, and the right information, many children in this condition go on to live healthy and productive lives.*
>
> *We are continually amazed at how much Jordan is growing every day and while many of you cannot see her daily, please know she continues to be a happy and loved little girl.*
>
> *For now, we don't need anything. (Although we love cookies.) As always, we feel your support and love. We cannot wait to see you all. We love you.*
>
> *Zachary and Leah*

Jordan's tiny whimper reminded us it was bedtime. There were routines to follow. Jordan still curled on Zac's lap to read *You Are My I Love You* before bedtime. She still let me sing "Neverland" before placing her in her crib, just as we had done every night for almost two years. I rubbed her back and looked around the room we had so carefully constructed for her. A nursery decorated with help from our friends, who had assisted in building the crib and applying owl stickers to the wall before Jordan was born. Homemade painted letters with her initials, painstaking details of love and support. A place representing the community the entire family had to lean on. Before leaving, I made sure she could see Joy, the owl, wherever she looked.

Lying in bed that night, I was reminded of the evening we found out Jacquie had died. When time has physical weight and falling asleep is an impossibility.

"Zac," I whispered.

"Yeah."

"What are you thinking?"

"I don't know how I'm going to do this. I don't know if I'm going to be a good enough dad to get her everything she is going to need."

I needed his honesty. I sat up and brushed a curl out of his face. "I know. Me too."

We sat there silently. When I asked him years later about that evening, he said he had been thinking about what the doctor had said about couples separating and how important it was for us to stay together. When you consider how much pressure is put on two people, it is no surprise how many relationships buckle.

But for that night, we didn't talk about us, our marriage, or the pressure. We just tried to get some sleep. After all, Jordan didn't know we were in the middle of a family crisis. She was going to need her mushy oatmeal first thing in the morning.

He took a breath. "Let's try to get some sleep."

"I'm not sure I can," I confessed. When I struggle to calm my brain, Zac gives me something relaxing to think about. It usually involves mentally reorganizing closets.

"Think about her laugh. Her silliness."

If I were in a ship that felt like it was sinking, I was glad he was in it with me.

I don't remember a lot about the following morning, except I yelled at my second-period class because three of them did not do their homework. It is one of the three times in my career I have raised my voice: the other two were for blatant bullying. I broke into a teacher tirade, lecturing them about how it was a gift that they could read, and they should appreciate that they had been given the ability. It was a disservice to their education that they were not using what they were capable of. It was unacceptable not to try; these were not the values of this classroom. The speech was longer than necessary, I banged on a table for impact, and I circled the same three points until my co-teacher gently stepped in to redirect the lesson. When we released the students forty minutes later, she let me cry it out for a hard four minutes, until the bell rang before the next class. Then, as I had learned to do, I swallowed it up, and I led the next class through a lesson on characterization.

The months that followed felt like a poorly designed movie montage, occurring in slow motion, underwater. Wash, rinse, repeat.

Ironically, the only reason I didn't break was that the weight of responsibility kept me buoyant. There was a little girl to take care of. There was a full-time job, laundry, and bills. There was a wonderful man to come home to who was just as dysregulated as I was. I found that if I jumped between the clouds of support of our family and friends, I could pretend I was staying afloat. Yet my responsibilities as a mother were also allowing me to live on my island of denial. In any other life's trauma, I would swerve into the sadness. Lie in bed under my covers, cry it out, and know that someone else would take care of my responsibilities. I could push on the bruise until the pain diminished. With this diagnosis, I did not find an opportunity to pause and process.

There was always a dull ache behind my eyes and an acorn planted in my stomach that could have sprouted into despair, but I refused to let it grow. I would not nourish it by talking about what I was feeling. Rather, I starved it by living only on the surface. But even if you squelch something that is supposed to bloom, it will find other ways to come out.

Our mail began to overflow. We were surrounded by a lot of love. The sentiments were similar.

"God wouldn't give you more than you could handle. He must know you are a strong family."

Inside a condolence card, "We are so sorry to hear your news. She has a beautiful face."

I recognized that no one knew what to say, and I appreciated the attempts, but they weren't quite helping. One, though, provided tools in my language: "You must read the poem 'Welcome to Holland' by Emily Perl Kingsley. It uses a metaphor to talk about what it feels like to be a special needs parent. You are a teacher; you like metaphors. I promise it will help."

It would take me years to realize my sorrow was a result of the shared cultural discussion around disabilities. There was an inherent message that stories of disabilities needed to be sad. When you had a member of your family with significant needs, it was something to mourn. These are individuals in society that are often relegated and live in the periphery. I was kind to the neighborhood girl with Down syndrome, but never saw her because she went to a different school. I heard people gently whisper about the boy with cerebral palsy in the community, but I never spoke to him. While I studied how to support diverse learners as a teacher, society taught me that, as a mother, it should be heartbreaking.

I appreciated every comment from my family and friends. Saying not quite the right thing is better than silence. However, I have since learned the words I needed to hear then and frequently remind myself of some of them now: "This is life-altering news, so take your time to process it. Remember to be kind to yourself; whatever you are feeling is valid, and there is no need to add guilt to it. It does not make you any less of a person that your emotions run the gamut from raging to regretful; in fact, it makes you even more human. And while it doesn't seem like it today, you will feel like yourself again; you may even laugh. Give yourself a break; you aren't made up of robot parts. Find people who will sit with you in your discomfort, invite you to feel it, and listen without trying to fix it. You will find your community; you do not have to do any of this alone."

CHAPTER 9
It's Never About the Shoes

To be a parent is to be flexible. It starts the moment you learn morning sickness is a misnomer, as your nausea usurps your dinner plans. You can plan all you want, but parenthood inevitably changes that course. Your child's rare diagnosis is one of these changes you can never anticipate. So you resort to crisis mode, where it is encouraged to respond quickly. It was pretty innate for me to move at this pace, so after Jordan's diagnosis, I overdid the response time and reverted back to my childhood mode.

It is a running joke in my family that my maiden name, Witman, is synonymous with a verb. If you "Witman" something, your weekend was perhaps filled with a hockey game on a Friday night, followed by a trip to Atlantic City the next morning, meeting the family for brunch at noon, re-mulching the backyard, seeing a movie, and still being in bed by six p.m. on a Saturday night. That was the pace of my retirement-age parents. The gene has really manifested itself quite powerfully in the younger generation. We're tornadoes.

I was moving fast long before the days of parenthood and, with Jordan, leaving the house became an Olympic sport. My ability to multitask-while-talking-on-the-phone-and-filling-out-paperwork-and-preparing-dinner was quite helpful for my current life situation.

If Jordan napped, I had exactly one hour to tackle my organizational missions: fold six baskets of laundry, clean the entire basement, or file every photo since puberty. Sure enough, she would start crying before the hour was up, so I'd sit and watch *Peppa Pig* for the tenth time, feeling despondent. I was so close to getting something done, and yet there I was, feeling unsatisfied with my hand in the box of cheddar crackers—again.

When I would get this way, Zac, who had a naturally calm disposition, liked to remind me of Wady, the kindhearted airport attendant, who we met on our first trip to Texas.

That first trip to meet my "even-though-we-aren't-dating,-I-am-in-love-with-your-son-and-I-hope-one-day-you-will-be" future in-laws, we were informed that, despite our delayed flight, our luggage might have previously arrived. When we landed in Dallas, I approached a man with a friendly face, khaki pants, and a name tag that read: *Wady*.

Me: Hello, Wady. We just got off the delayed flight from Newark, and we were wondering if you could tell us where our luggage is.

Wady: Ma'am. I'm gonna have to ask you to *calm* down. [Insert arm gesture for: *Hope I can relax this crazy East Coast lady with all the hair.*]

Me: Oh, no. I'm not upset. I-was-just-wondering-where-we-could-locate-our-luggage-because-we-don't-know-where-to-find-it. They-told-us-it-might-be-at-the-baggage-claim-or-maybe—

Wady: Ma'am, I'm gonna need you to *calm* down.

We tried back and forth a few more times and then both helplessly turned to our interpreter. Luckily, my (I-hope-you-realize-how-much-you-love-me-on-this-trip) travel companion was a native Texan who now lived in New York City and could translate for us.

Handsome Travel Companion: We are looking for our bags, sir.

Wady: Carousel three.

I will never forget Wady. He became our code to slow down, even long before we had children.

But I never really could stop moving. I was in the working-full-time-mommy-grade-shower-eat mode, and it seemed like it was working for me.

Until it didn't.

A few months after Jordan's diagnosis, we were having family errand time. I was accustomed to Jersey mall shopping, so I found needing to make several stops a hassle. But we found an efficient way to spend time together and get errands done at the same time. One of us would stay in the car with Jordan, and the other would pop out to get what we needed. It was my turn to go inside. I was picking up broken shoes I had dropped off over a year ago. The shoemaker in our town is a sweet elderly man, who waves his hand and says, "Ah, you pay me next time." I don't know how he stays in business. I also don't know why I suddenly thought it was important to get these shoes I hardly wore, but alas, it was on the family errand list.

When I walked in, I gave the man the ticket for my shoes. I can't find my glasses on a daily basis, but somehow, I could find this random receipt. He searched his inventory and told me he did not have the shoes.

"But I dropped them off, and I have the ticket," I declared.

"We haven't used that color ticket in a long time. I don't think your shoes are here."

Perhaps the conversation went on longer, but I weakly muttered "okay" and walked out. When I opened the car door, I burst into tears. "He can't find my shoes."

"Which pair was it?" Zac said with concern on his face.

"I don't remember. But he lost them." Then I started wailing.

Zac drove the mile to our house while I vented about this sweet man. It probably sounded something like this: "They created the ticket system. I didn't make up that ticket. I have been holding onto this ticket for so long. Did they give my shoes away? I will never get to wear them again. I was supposed to pick them up. It was on the list, and now I can't cross it off."

We pulled into the driveway, and he turned to me with a loving smile on his face. He took my hands and said gently, "Leah. This isn't about the shoes."

I sniffled with a heaving chest. "Yeah, probably."

I'm grateful he acknowledged what was below the surface. It was the first time either of us had. Honestly, I wasn't going to slow down long enough to reflect on what was happening. Speed had become my new method of denial. But no matter how-fast-I-moved-throughout-the-day making new schedules and plans, it wasn't going to change my child's prognosis. She still had cri du chat. She still may never walk, and I had to begin to learn it was out of my control.

I didn't have time for that. I didn't want to find my inner Wady and talk about it. I wouldn't let myself slow down. If I paused, I couldn't control what would pour out of me, and I didn't think I would restart again.

I knew I was not helping anyone. Not myself, not my child, and certainly not my marriage. I have read the statistics for divorced parents of special needs children. I get how it happens. You move from being a couple in a relationship to just nice people who are parenting each other's child. There is nothing wrong; there is just no time and truly little control.

We did try where we could. Zac is better at it and I did my best to follow his lead. I watched him sip his morning cup of coffee in complete silence, even if it meant waking up at 4:00 a.m. before Jordan's early rising. He is comforted by an organized dishwasher and planning his next barbecue smoke-out. I momentarily escape into a good book or find a new project to organize. After the next inevitable day of moving-impossibly-fast, I would try to remember to put on some music and make space in my closet for the shoes I still chose to wear.

CHAPTER 10
Mrs. Doubtfire

We found a new childcare setting that assured us they could accommodate Jordan's needs; therapists would be able to work with her in an individualized space, and the remainder of the day she could focus on socialization. We would drop her off on our way to work, prepared with her backup clothes, snacks, and backpack of materials (she had more homework than my high school students did).

By the end of the first week, we learned that while the other children sat at the table for their snack, Jordan was left in her adaptable chair on the floor, completely alone. "We thought she would be safer down there," they told us.

Then she got kicked out. "We don't think we can meet her needs. Her schedule is too demanding for us."

We were at a loss. I wanted to give up and quit my job. "Finding a good day care for Jordan seems impossible. She has so many therapists to fit in. Maybe one of us should stay home," I suggested.

It took a lot of soul-searching to realize we weren't best suited to be Jordan's caretakers either. Parents, yes, but organizers of the transitions and therapy—no. My husband and I love teaching, but ironically, we wouldn't be great teachers for Jordan. My strengths were to discuss social justice literature, not the pincer grasp (which I thought was the *pincher* grasp). At her first whimper, I would insist the therapist reconvene the next day. A request they politely ignored. It was clear: we needed to find someone else to help.

Thus, the search for the world's perfect babysitter began, directly out of the script of *Mrs. Doubtfire*. In the meantime, we called in all favors to watch Jordan: both sets of grandparents, my sister, neighbors, former students, the mailman.

Applicant A: I have extensive work with special needs children. I have a master's degree in education. I require a salary of $120,000 a year plus benefits.

Applicant B: I am great with kids. A lot of times, I take off my wigs and let the kids play with them. I find that is the most entertaining toy of all.

Applicant C: Your house is too messy for me. [Note: one sock on the floor] I would insist you change the way you store the food in your fridge. I would make her schedule. She doesn't need the therapies you describe.

Applicant D: I love kids. I babysat throughout high school and I am majoring in education in college now. Yes, I do have a current job, but I can just not go. I do that all the time. Oh, my job? I'm in the food industry. Hooters. Here are some of my modeling shots.

By the time we got to *Applicant N,* we found her. Lisa entered the house and sat on the floor next to our daughter during the interview. She gently picked up a toy and waited to make eye contact. We didn't need to choose her, because Jordan did. Lisa quickly became our LaLa.

The next day, the cover story on the news discussed a young nanny who had brutally killed two small children. There was no way I was going to work—ever again.

When I had been pregnant, my friend sent me this Elizabeth Stone quote: "Making the decision to have a child—it's momentous. It is to decide forever to have your heart go walking around outside your body." I never understood the force of those words until that moment. I had spent so long cradling this heart; how could I possibly now leave her with a stranger? It was different in my house than it was with the childcare. It felt easier to steal just one baby than it did to pack up ten to fifteen of them.

I had to trust that our instincts (and references) were right; LaLa was not a serial killer but truly as incredible as she seemed. I once again kissed Jordan goodbye and worked through my sea of tears to perform my daily tasks. Leaving Jordan felt impossible, but maybe this torment could help me find a friend. I couldn't connect with most parents; discussing your child's microcephaly isn't much of a crowd-pleaser, as most parents aren't well-versed in the implications of decreased head circumference, but it seemed like a universal pain of parenthood to leave your child for the day. Maybe, when I floated to the surface again, I could use this as a starting idea to finally meet my neighbors.

Day after day I kept walking out the door. The change in Jordan was noticeable within weeks. She would reach out her hand to gesture for help, not in my direction, but for LaLa. I was not hurt by this, but rather grateful for the partnership. There was someone else invested in helping us care for our child and her extraordinary needs. It was the beginning of the breather we so desperately needed. We had an expert who facilitated a thirty-hour therapy schedule, supported Jordan, and surprised us with homemade pot pie.

Although Lisa relocated and no longer works with Jordan daily, the impact she left on our house is permanent. Years later, I still find evidence of her dedication to Jordan's development: a picture schedule created to allow Jordan to successfully transition between her intensive therapy sessions, a photo of her first army crawl. Lisa was there when Jordan received her new leg orthotics that fell just below her knees and showed her how to strike a pose while wearing them. Lisa was there teaching our child how to access the world and modeling for us how gracefully it could be done.

CHAPTER 11
Dear Woman at the
Grocery Store

Well, good morning. I see you noticing my child, sucking on a pink lollipop at 7:00 a.m., watching *Yo Gabba Gabba!* on her tablet. I see you trying not to give me the "mommy judgmental eyes," instead making it look like you are smiling at how cute she is with her pajama bottoms, one shoe, and a sweater with chocolate on it. I know you aren't referring to your newly read mommy manual that discusses appropriate behavior for children in public but assessing how poorly my performance would rank.

We are here because our ice pop box has a lovely picture showing three vibrant ice pops in blue, red, and purple. My little one has learned to say the word "purple." She proudly and slowly states, "pur-ple." This has taken six months to learn with the support of three therapists with master's degrees.

There are only two purple ice pops in each box. I now have forty blue and red ice pops filling my freezer and just cleaned up one small child who was having a meltdown on the floor. So I won't respond to your look to tell you we are here for a new box. I won't tell you my daughter took fifteen minutes to transition into the car because she was having sensory overload issues that made her bite my arm and kick my husband. I won't tell you that the pink lollipop is being used to soothe her overstimulation. I won't tell you that her orthotics were rubbing her feet in the car so badly that she screamed and pulled them off herself, or that this sweater is the only one she will wear this week—despite how late we stay up doing laundry. I also won't inform you that the tablet is an educational tool that she has learned to navigate and will perhaps be her speaking device to communicate with the entire world. Without this tablet on her lap, she will probably try to rip all the labels off the shelves. After spending eight hours in school and therapy yesterday, she deserves a little downtime. And shopping without her yelling is like a trip to a day spa for me.

Instead, I will smile, say, "Excuse me," and grab our treat.

CHAPTER 12
How to Make an Exquisite List

First, you choose the perfect-sized piece of paper. I prefer mine to be in a lined notebook, college ruled, none of this wide business. Then I draw tiny boxes next to each item on my to-do list. The satisfaction of checking them off is enough to appease even the most overscheduled, choice-fatigued caregiver. The real secret is to add items you have already accomplished, just so you can cross them off. It starts the day with a real win. It also helps to slow me down.

TO-DO LIST FOR FEBRUARY 2, 2013
- ❏ Microwave frozen chicken tacos
- ❏ Shower
- ❏ Grade poetry assignments
- ❏ Write holiday thank-you notes
- ❏ Breathe

The to-do list helped me ride the wave of the post-diagnosis days. I didn't really ride as much as hold on and awkwardly slap against the water. I received incredible support during the first two years of Jordan's life and now she was beginning to pull herself up to stand, but

I was still not taking care of myself. If it didn't make it to the to-do list, it was not getting completed. I would sacrifice sleep and friendships if I could read more about the PROMPT method for speech therapy, designed to produce more sounds from Jordan's mouth. I ignored the rules of my healthy, nutritional diet to learn more about a sensory diet, daily activities designed to help with Jordan's adaptive responses. And with twenty pounds—okay, thirty—added to my frame, I convinced myself I was killing this juggling act. Screw my pep talk. I *was* made of robot parts. The reality was that Zac and I could juggle everything that needed to be juggled ... except ourselves. We couldn't find a surplus of energy to focus on our marriage, our friendships, or our individuality. I was happy to put myself last: not enough salmon for dinner—I'll just eat ice cream. Couldn't accept the invitation from friends because of Jordan's schedule—I wasn't up for much company anyway. Basic self-care—my fifteen-dollar manicure would just chip anyway, and the money saved could buy Jordan a new squishy sensory ball. I could revisit a childhood hobby, but recording original songs on my Fisher-Price boom box felt a bit too 1980s. I could try to connect with some other parents, but then I would have to put on real pants.

Nothing was exactly wrong, except it was not the life we had imagined for ourselves. We had been dealing with so many serious issues, we didn't know how to find levity, despite the continual efforts from our cheering section. We would have momentary relief when friends visited from Brooklyn, my sister arranged a virtual playdate with my niece, or care packages arrived in the mail. On one occasion, it was a gigantic container of jelly beans; another, a heartfelt card celebrating our strength. Each gesture was appreciated, provided a brief respite, and needed another thank-you card I forgot to write. When a gigantic pillow arrived with a photo of our friends in a ridiculous pose, underneath a rainbow of iridescent sequins, we placed it in the center of the couch to remind us that playfulness was something we needed to work for, without having to concretely record it.

TO-DO LIST FOR APRIL 10, 2013
- ❑ Schedule Jordan's surgery for her ear tubes
- ❑ Find plain white socks for orthotics
- ❑ Clarify the co-pays on the insurance forms
- ❑ Shower?
- ❑ Date night: fall asleep on couch

The marriage, at its core, was happy. We were still us; we had the foundation of our friendship to thank for that. The effervescence of our twenties had become muted. The passion of the relationship that had started it all, sadly, now came last. This lack of energy was a sign of how safe we were in our relationship. Just as Jordan would make it through an entire day with therapists and only crumble when she was safe in our loving arms, we would hold ourselves together all day and only deflate when we could sit kid-free, depleted, zoning out on the couch. We tried to chat, but it was more energy than we could muster. She also might wake up screaming from yet another ear infection, and we wouldn't be able to sit long anyway.

My father called with a gentle observation. "You need a change of scenery. Go somewhere. We will watch Jordan," he advised. "You should always have something to look forward to."

We ignored our pragmatic tendencies and used our allocated funds for a small trip, just two days. It would be good for Jordan too; she deserved fresh enthusiasm with her eager-to-babysit grandparents. We approached the decision of where to travel as a chipper young couple, not with the recent drudgery of our days. We determined that if we were going to remember how to be humans again, we needed a momentary break from parenthood. I needed to travel somewhere without constantly checking in. It needed to be out of the country.

With the privilege of air miles, a support system, and a knowledge of London, we packed up our passports, boarding passes, and backpacks smaller than the work bag I carried every day, and set off—for forty-eight hours. When the plane started, the thud of the door felt like the umbilical cord was being ripped from my body. I spent the entire flight holding my silenced phone, listing all the reasons this trip was a terrible idea. I was not cultivating anything even remotely close to romance.

The plane landed, we collapsed in our hotel room, and I took a shower. The first one in three years without fear of what was happening on the other side of the door. I even shaved my legs—both of them. When I turned my neck to grab a washcloth, I heard a gigantic crunch of vertebrae, a familiar and jarring sound. It did not feel like a release of tension, but a warning sign of what had been building up. Ten minutes strolling through the archives of the British Library allowed my shoulders to release from my ears. An afternoon in Covent Garden unzipped me from the seriousness of our lives. An evening in a dim theater jump-started our laughter as we found ourselves blending in with strangers' cackles. We sauntered. We sipped. We reconnected to being ourselves again. I even had a rare glass of wine. Zac and I actually talked to each other, and, more importantly, we listened; turned out, he was still funny.

When we called from a pay phone to check in on Jordan, my mother calmly reported that Jordan had the stomach flu. *It's all under control. Enjoy your trip.* Then our money for the call ran out. Zac presented our options: head to the airport or trust my mom had it under control and see how many performance artists we could locate in South Bank.

The answer was four. The juggler reciting Shakespeare was my favorite. Within forty-eight hours, we were home. Life continued.

TO-DO LIST FOR MAY 10, 2013
- ❑ Microwave frozen pizza
- ❑ Shower
- ❑ Grade personal essays
- ❑ Write holiday thank-you notes

My father had been right: we did need something on the horizon to look forward to. We don't always have the time and resources for a jaunt across the pond, but a simple walk around a bookstore with just the two of us provides a much-needed break. Even a shared television show on the couch delivers an escape when we cannot physically have one.

Making lists suggests control, but nothing is as effective as real breathing space. And knowing that we have time to ourselves on the calendar—not just exhausted, end-of-the-day time, but purposeful time to unfasten our daily armor—reminds me to breathe. Sometimes even without putting it on a list.

CHAPTER 13
I Can Make It to the Mailbox

I hated running. I didn't mind it so much when I'd played soccer and I forgot I was technically running, but I really despised it when there was nothing to do *but* run. I had tried to exercise in college, but I inevitably found myself stopping on the side of the road, choreographing, and singing show tunes instead of increasing my heart rate. (I should see someone for my unresolved Broadway dreams.)

My roommate would encourage me. "Just to the mailbox, Leah. You can do it!" she would cheer. Her red hair flying in front of me. "You can do it!"

"I mean, we could—or we could stop at the Union and get some ice cream first?"

Running really wasn't my calling; in fact, I was envious of people who used it as an outlet. One friend runs miles every morning without music or a phone, and I couldn't imagine leaving my brain alone for that long. It would just highlight the feelings I was working so hard to avoid. We did keep a photo on our fridge of my father-in-law, Phil, running a marathon, along with a handwritten note: *Always finish life's tasks before they sweep up the Dixie cups*. It was a nice reminder that I could move at my own pace, but, still, I preferred that pace to be sipping tea and reading books.

This is why it was so surprising one afternoon when I randomly said to Zac, "I'll be right back; I need to go outside."

I threw on a pair of sneakers and temporarily gave myself a time-out from adulting. I just started walking down the street. I resembled Edward Scissorhands, bumbling down the center of the road, arms extended, no phone, no keys, no sports bra. And then, Forrest Gump style, I picked up my pace, suddenly running. I wasn't tired. I wasn't bored. I was outside—by myself.

When I clocked it later, I'd run more than two miles. And there was a hill. Yes, I was impressed too. I tried to recreate it later that week but realized the first time had simply been an aberration. With that second run, I just looked at the hill, turned around, and walked home belting, "Climb Every Mountain."

When I returned home that initial day, I tried to identify just what it was I was running from. And there it sat—the gait trainer. The fire-engine-red metal walker I had picked up a month ago to help Jordan learn to walk. She was two years old with a mouth full of teeth and a head of springy curls. She was delicious. Her new, pink, princess–patterned orthotics—her dancing shoes as we called them—extended from each knee down to her toes. They were designed to support her muscles so she could learn to stand. She had successfully learned to pull up, but her body couldn't seem to handle its own weight to maintain walking.

I had initially been excited to pick up her gait trainer. It functioned as a walker, allowing her to rest her weight on the metal frame while she wheeled across the floor. The experts didn't know if walking was a possibility, due to her hypotonia, and we were beginning to take measurements to see if the house could become wheelchair accessible. "Try the walker; see how she takes to it," the therapists encouraged.

When you have a child with significant developmental delays, you acquire a team to break down individual areas of need. In our case: experts in speech, occupational, physical, feeding, applied behavior analysis, and play therapy. They also work collaboratively to address the needs of the whole child. In some cases, this is joined with a family trainer, usually a social worker, who addresses the social-emotional needs of the child and the family. We would meet twice a month to brainstorm the next goal for Jordan. What exactly was causing the delay in walking? Was it that her muscles were too weak to support her body? Was it a cognitive disconnect that meant she did not understand how to motor plan to make walking possible? Was her constant wailing during physical therapy a result of fatigue, pain, or frustration?

It was the team that helped us shape our parenting philosophy. We had realistic expectations for what was possible, but maintained a sense of hope by looking ahead. Just because the diagnosis said *can't*, it didn't mean she *couldn't*.

The gait walker, upon sight, made Jordan recoil in fear and cry hysterically. I couldn't stand witnessing this fear and preferred to teach her arm choreography for *Flashdance* rather than practice. Zac was much better at working with her, so I focused my attention on color-coding her therapy schedule while they practiced. I watched the neighborhood children run through their backyards while I measured the distance of our kitchen to see if it could accommodate a wheelchair, just in case.

"Place your foot here, Jordan," Zac cheered over her wailing. "That's great, try to take a step."

We schlepped the walker to the park, the mall, and the playground. She was terrified every time. The therapists continued to brainstorm new techniques to motivate Jordan to increase her mobility. It appeared as if her body were ready for walking, but she was too afraid. Jordan's physical therapist and LaLa tried to redirect her. They moved her through space with hoops, banged on drums, and led her toward her toys. They stimulated her muscles with weighted tools and even tried treats to move toward. More recoiling and wailing. Our family trainer suggested inviting her therapy dog, Fozzie, into Jordan's session. Jordan had always loved touching Fozzie's snuggly fur, and it might do the trick.

We were at work when Jordan took her first independent steps, trying to grab Fozzie's tail. It did not matter. Her team knew they were witnessing something that had been deemed impossible. They knew to communicate their pride to her, to encourage her to keep trying, and to celebrate with a dance party.

Desperate to bottle this moment, Zac and I raced home and spent the afternoon coaxing Jordan to recreate what she had done, without the company of her canine companion. With her new confidence, she stretched out her arms, laughed hysterically, and took three timid steps toward us. That moment will always be for me what the movie *An Affair to Remember* is for my mother: it doesn't matter what I am doing; I will always tear up when I think about that day when my two-and-a-half-year-old daughter who wasn't supposed to walk started walking.

We immediately changed her into her favorite dress and took her outside for our first photo shoot. She loved an audience. We spent the afternoon ignoring all our responsibilities and celebrating her steps. Now, when you walk into our home, you will find a large photo of Jordan, age two-and-a-half, arms outstretched to the sky, celebrating her newfound independence.

A few weeks later, I found myself in a quiet moment while Jordan napped. "I'll be right back," I called to Zac. "I just need to go outside."

I strolled down the sidewalk. My thoughts were inundated with pride for my daughter. She had checked off the first box on her "Won't Be Able to Do" list. I started to pick up my pace.

If my daughter could learn to walk, surely I could make it to the mailbox.

CHAPTER 14
Finding Her Voice

Jordan had a lot to say; she just didn't know how to say it so other people could understand.

Since her diagnosis, we had inundated her with sign language. Jordan responded well to this form of communication. Her little fingers came together to ask for "more." A hand to the mouth to say "thank you," palms rubbed to ask for cheese, and a favorite homemade sign, a triangle above her forehead for strawberries. She still does this one when she eats her morning breakfast.

The three of us would curl up on the couch watching *Baby Signing Time* and imitate the gestures to learn how to communicate. When Rachel Coleman, the creator of the program, was the guest performer at that year's 5p- conference, we all lined up like we were at a rock concert. "More," Jordan signed, touching her little fingers together when the concert finished. "More."

At two, we enrolled her in a developmental day-care program to increase her support and interaction with other children. It was here we learned the development of language broke down into expressive and receptive communication. Jordan's receptive language was improving, meaning she could understand us, but her expressive language was still in the 1 percent margin, so she would require accommodations to speak. We were trained with the Picture Exchange Communication System (PECS), a communication method that taught her how to hand a single picture of a desired item to her partner, who would fulfill the request. If she signed for "music," we would turn to the page with the three images for the nursery rhymes she liked and allow her to choose: star ("Twinkle, Twinkle"), farmer ("Old MacDonald"), or boat ("Row, Row, Row Your Boat"). Even when she touched the star for the tenth consecutive time, we were thrilled, because it was her choice.

We continued to advance in our practice and began using an tablet to access a new touch-to-talk program. When she touched the corresponding picture, the computer would talk for her and she could hear her request aloud. Jordan would place two fingers to her mouth— "hungry." We would hand her the program and she would select a picture from the list of fruit.

"Banana!"

She would laugh. There was a little fault to the system. Jordan didn't like to eat bananas as much as she liked the sound of the word. In fact, she liked it so much, she would hit the button consecutively, and we would spend our meals listening to a computerized voice rap "banana" in the background.

Then she developed a language only she understood. I called it the "outline of words." She produced the beginning of a sound, but the middle was missing, so the sounds were incomprehensible. Like all children acquiring language, she looked at the lips of a person speaking and imitated the sounds she heard coming from their mouth. She cognitively processed sounds and words differently, so she would have entire conversations, monologues, epic poems for just herself. They were hysterical, perhaps something about balloons, elephants, armpits—maybe eBay. Whatever she was saying, we were coached to continue the conversation—"Really! That's wonderful, Jordan!"—to which she would proudly smile. Our background as theater educators makes this perpetual improvisational game successful. This type of language was exhilarating because we learned she was interested, expressive, and, most importantly—happy.

Then she began her *approximations*, the clinical term for starting a word. It became a game.

Red-faced Jordan would begin, "Bbbbb."

We would look around the room to see what object might begin with a "B."

"Do you want a banana, honey? Bagel? Bassoon?"

She would giggle and point.

"Banana! Good girl!"

She still wouldn't eat it, but she'd proudly identified it. Her incredible speech therapists would slowly progress these approximations into larger utterances, one word at a time. Their work was nothing short of magic.

Slowly, she spoke. Small, carefully chosen words she had been practicing. First, she would point at the corresponding photos in books, repeat them, study them, and then, one day, claim them as her own. The speech therapist chose strategic and purposeful words to get her through her day: "ba-na-na."

An unfamiliar listener may not have understood it, but to us, it was music. I imagine that every parent experiences this sensation when their baby starts to tell them what they are thinking. Jordan's identification of the banana was the equivalent of a college acceptance letter.

On the morning of my thirty-third birthday, she was playing with her pretend food. I kissed her on the forehead as I headed out to work, the same way I did every day. In her world, Mommy only went two places anyway: to work and to pee pee.

"Bye, little one. Mommy is going to work. Have a great day. I love you."

Her calculated, little voice replied carefully, "I. Love. You."

I called for Zac to listen and, sure enough, she looked up from the plastic piece of pizza, smiled proudly at her doting parents, and repeated a phrase she had heard daily for the past three years of her life. "Love. You." Her voice was tiny, high-pitched, and perfect.

She didn't stop there. Four-year-old Jordan and I were driving home from a routine checkup, and she called for my attention. "Mama." I caught her eye in the rearview mirror and saw she was pointing to a picture of two hearts.

"Mama heart. Jordan heart."

"Yes, honey. That could be both of our hearts," I encouraged.

All that talk of "never." Never sharing her ideas, never speaking in sentences. It was never expected that she would say something so beautiful, it could be its own form of poetry.

"Your heart perfect for my heart." Then she pointed across the page. "Mama cow go moo."

The moment was simple and finished.

I will never know what prompted this connection between us and the two symmetrical hearts. Maybe she absorbed all the nights I read her "[i carry your heart with me (i carry it in]" by e. e. cummings. Maybe Elmo had taught her about unwavering love. Whatever the case, she was right. Our hearts were perfect for each other, and she worked tirelessly to express love, regardless of the form.

Take that, cri du chat.

CHAPTER 15
Birthday Party Favors

Walk: check. Talk: check, check.

Jordan was proving to be quite a fighter.

We wanted to see if we could help her facilitate some friendships. Many of her words were unintelligible, so people had a hard time understanding what she was saying. Still, she was making great progress in speech therapy to articulate her initial sounds, she never minded repeating herself, and she knew how to give clues to help make her meaning clear (she pantomimed the game Simon Says to tell me the new boy in class was named Simon).

It also helped that Jordan was a naturally social person—her teacher voted her most likely to be "mayor" because she was always smiling to her "townspeople" as she walked up and down the hallways. It was here she started a lifelong habit, blowing kisses to her image in any reflective surface. Time for physical therapy—let me kiss that face in the water fountain first. Can't start music class until we wave enthusiastically to the reflection in the classroom door. She performed beautiful duets with her own shadow. It seemed like a girl this confident would naturally love having some other people to talk to.

We had become so insular in taking care of her needs, we hadn't cultivated any relationships with other parents of families, partially because Jordan was fearful anywhere out of her routine. Zac reached out to our applied behavior analysis therapist for strategies to confront situations that were harrowing for her. We didn't want to overextend her, but if we could also get back into the world, it might benefit all of us. We wanted her to gain comfort in situations that generally caused her to melt down. We identified three specific spaces: large crowds, anywhere "Happy Birthday" was sung, and, eventually, the school bus.

It seemed impossible to achieve any of these goals. Even at the cri du chat convention, which we chose to attend that year, Jordan was the only child there who was fearful about entering the large tent for the evening celebration. There was just too much stimulus and it took over an hour to transition her into the space. Parent after parent gave us suggestions, but nothing worked. We could have just gone home, but she had previously been excited about going in. Her body language had told us. We were also desperate for a night to talk with other families. When we finally wore her down and she was too tired to fight it, we collapsed into our seats and watched some of the older kids dance. Another mom, who had seen us in the doorway, came over to commiserate. For her son, it was ceiling fans. Her therapist told the family to avoid them for years, but she didn't think that was practical. Instead, she took him to Home Depot every day for a month and pushed him up and down the ceiling fan aisle in a cart until he was desensitized. I loved this story, the image of a mom sauntering down the aisle while her son screamed, a little less each time. I knew I didn't have the tenacity for it, especially in places with large crowds that were not as understanding as those at this convention. We determined it was best to start with the practical: birthday parties. All three-year-olds loved cake.

We first attempted the birthday party of the child of a friend from graduate school. She is a very understanding person; we knew there would be no guilt or judgment if attending the party turned out to be a colossal disaster. I called ahead and explained the circumstances to her, and she not only provided the details of the party but also the exact layout of the day's events. One day after work, I drove over to the facility, took pictures on my phone for Jordan, and created a personalized social story—an album of photos—to help Jordan know what to expect. This strategy provides visual cues for the exact process Jordan can prepare for. We found she was more successful if we showed her real photos, rather than clip art, which we would print onto a sheet of paper, laminate, and use to guide us through any new activity. It was a manageable strategy and also a great excuse to purchase a laminator—a teacher's dream. In this case, we had six photos: the outfit she would wear, our car, the entrance to the building, the birthday girl's face, the cake, and our car again for the ride home. A week later, we returned with Jordan for a practice run, using the social story to guide her through the space before it would be filled with joyful children.

On the day of the party, Jordan was dressed in her favorite pink cupcake dress, just as we had practiced. As Zac drove, we reviewed the social story to discuss the upcoming steps. But when we stepped into the party room, her fear won. Perhaps the chairs were in a different location or the noise was still too loud, but it took both Zac and me to restrain her. Flailing arms, punching fists, wailing. She was afraid.

I know we should have left immediately, but we recalled the story of the ceiling fans and how it's possible to become desensitized to your fears. Perhaps we needed to push her a little out of her comfort zone. Of course, my friend would understand, there would be other parties, but we were also desperate to participate in that typical world of small talk, cake, goody bags. We ultimately left, defeated, after forty-five minutes. Despite all our strategies, there was nothing we could do to calm Jordan down.

We had learned, even when we faced setbacks, to compliment every effort Jordan made to try something new. That way, next time, we could push her further.

Upon our return to the car, her tears stopped immediately and mine started. It was one thing to be able to communicate with others and run on a playground, but if we couldn't be social, I was worried I would implode. I missed being with other people.

"Jordan, we are so proud of you for going to the party," I spoke into the rearview mirror.

"Party!" She smiled.

"Oh." My husband and I looked at each other. "You had fun," I repeated.

"Yes."

"Oh, good. Maybe we will go to another one, honey," Zac reassured her.

With each invitation, I would call and ask the parent the same favor: "Could you provide the details of the location and a schedule for the event?" Jordan would squeeze into the same cupcake dress for as long as it fit, and we would try again.

For the next one, we made it into the room. Party number three, we played near another child. Party number four, we sat for pizza and, ultimately, stayed through the singing of "Happy Birthday," despite covering our ears with headphones. It was always hard for her, but we made it a family effort to try.

We worked through this birthday party aversion for her own celebrations too. We just adjusted to keep her comfortable. We would sing "Twinkle, Twinkle" instead of "Happy Birthday." We had a pajama dance party with her cousin, Abigail, in the quiet of our house. She invited a few classmates to a dance studio. She wasn't fearful of her own party—the secret was presents.

When she was six, Jordan was invited to the ultimate challenge birthday party: the bouncy house. Her low muscle tone made this an especially difficult setting. But on this day, she was determined to scale the "Great Slide." To be successful, she would have to independently run up the side, cling to a small handle, and propel herself to the top. I wasn't going to stop her, but it seemed challenging, even for me. She bravely tried it by herself first. With each ensuing attempt, she still couldn't make it to the first stair, but she was not going to be discouraged.

She ran over. "Mama, help."

I was particularly exhausted that day. I looked longingly at the other parents bantering while their children independently bounced. Zac would have been far more successful at this request, but I saw her hopeful face as she stood in her cupcake dress, now a crop top. It was not too long ago we wouldn't have even made it into the building. I took off my shoes. *We've got this*, I thought.

I positioned her in front of me. We allowed some tiny toddlers to scoot past us. We took a running leap and immediately slipped our way back to the beginning. Undeterred, she was back up.

This is a child who does not understand the word "no." Not because of her receptive language delays, but because she has always been a fighter. The experts were right: years of Early Intervention services and nurturing therapists had created a space where Jordan comfortably pushed herself. I was often the one who wanted to stop when she cried too hard or seemed too fatigued—not her. Jordan had internalized resilience through the countless hours she sat at the dining room table, practicing her strategies and patiently hearing each therapist's rally cry: "Good start, Jordan, try again."

This time it was her turn to push me.

"Again."

The second time, I had a new plan. If I guided her toward the top while maintaining my own footing, we could both be successful. The connection to parenting was not lost on me—I must steady myself first to support her. Despite some rope burn and a small child landing on my head, we both remained laughing. We might not get up this bouncy slide, but we sure were having fun trying. Attempt three, four, five.

"Again."

On the next running start, I learned if I carried her and dug my feet into the sides, we could get farther than we had last time. Thanks to the practice I had carrying her growing body, I was strong enough to get us both to the first handle.

"I do it!"

We were attracting a cheering squad. The parents of her classmates were below, encouraging us to keep trying. We were finally at the top of the slide. It may as well have been Mount Rushmore. Jordan stood at the top, spun, and blew kisses to her adoring crowd. Her trademark moves.

I was ready for some water and a bench. This parenting thing was hard.

"Mama? Again."

CHAPTER 16
Party of Five

The decision to have our first child had never been a decision. Zac and I had always known we wanted a family. We also wanted to see how much curly hair our baby would have. The decision to continue to expand our family was a much larger conversation.

The topic surfaced when Jordan was almost two years old. She had started walking and had begun to develop more language. I wanted her speech to improve; when she shouted "Hi, old lady!" at a stranger, I wasn't upset that the woman didn't understand her. Her behaviors were momentarily under control and we understood her therapy schedule. Balanced meals occurred, where vegetables replaced Chinese comfort takeout. I even started to wear pants that weren't just drawstring—most of the time. It became the moment to address the conversation.

Genetic testing revealed Zac was a carrier for cri du chat. He had a balanced translocation, meaning his fifth and seventh chromosomes were switched, but no deletions were present. The clearest explanation I give to people is to picture a black pen with a red top and a red pen with a black top (I am clearly not a scientist). Because it was linked to his genes, they decided to expand testing for his family. We learned that his sister, Amanda, had the opposite of what Jordan had. In short, geneticists love our family. It meant there were three outcomes for future children: typical chromosomes, balanced translocation, or unbalanced translocation.

We sat down to eat dinner, Jordan sitting between us in her therapist-approved Tripp Trapp chair, which we'd luckily found on a special needs parents' site. While we discussed our options, and made sure Jordan fully swallowed each bite of her chicken before she took the next, Zac tried to make sense of the test results.

He didn't express his feelings with words as much as exhalations. When he had sorted his feelings, he said, "Guilt. I feel guilt."

"Well, you are also the reason she is stunning. I mean, those cheekbones did not come from my side of the family."

But I knew this was not something to make light of. With all of these emotions, I never once felt angry with Zac. I made a silly face at Jordan. I was never quite sure what she understood, but if I had relaxed body language and made her laugh, it kept her calm—which meant we could have the hard conversations in real time.

He explained the guilt he felt was for me, as his wife. In his mind, these were his genes, which means he could have had a child with a disability regardless of who he married; but if I had married someone else, my chances would have been smaller. "I'm just sorry you have to deal with this because you married me. It's sewn into me, but for you, it's a choice," he confessed.

Maybe because I remembered every moment of what it felt like to be near him during our days at NYU, maybe because Zac was the first and only person I fell in love with, or maybe because I had seen him handle stress that no son or father should face, the only response I had to his loving confession was, "I love you." I would rather have this life with him than any other life with anyone else.

After a bit more discussion, we made our decision. We would see what our options were to have another child. Was it practical? Having Jordan had already restructured our entire universe. How could we take care of her *and* a newborn? What if that child also had a disability? Forty hours a week of Early Intervention services, year-round schooling—and unlimited doctor appointments after school, not to mention our full-time jobs—was already taxing. Was there enough money to support another kid, beyond the special needs trust we'd established for Jordan, and an absurd amount of diapers? We still had to update our will to make sure someone could take care of her if we couldn't. We were planning for her entire life while she slept in a portable crib. Was it fair to imagine another child beside her?

It wasn't that we were unfulfilled as parents; it was just the opposite. We had learned how incredible it was to raise a child and celebrate the simple occurrences in life. However, Zac and I couldn't quiet the voices that raising Jordan with a sibling could be beneficial for her. Jordan could watch her sibling's development and perhaps learn from him or her. We could be a family that had a child with special needs rather than have it be our only defining factor. Another baby could help take care of Jordan as she got older and protect her when Mommy and Daddy weren't around. That was a lot of pressure to put on an imagined fetus, and I wasn't quite sure how I felt about it.

We focused on what we knew. We had learned as parents to be ready for the unexpected. A potential baby would have to navigate atypical circumstances, but there was nothing dire about the situation. Jordan was not someone we needed to hide, to protect another child from. She would be a very loving sibling. This was not the time to make a pros-and-cons list, as I might have for so many other decisions. We knew we were ready, and we followed our gut. We were going to try to expand our family.

When Jordan was older, she explained to us how babies are born. She explained that Mommy and Daddy have a true love story and then babies danced in their stomachs and said, "Ta-da, magic, I'm here."

We wished it were that simple. For our family, in vitro fertilization (IVF) preimplantation screening was recommended to identify the genetic makeup of the embryos. After engaging in the IVF process, a cell is removed from the embryo and tested to see if there is a specific genetic condition (in our case, a deletion of the fifth chromosome) before transferring the embryo to the uterus. We read paperwork about risks, rights, and responsibilities. We did not make this decision lightly.

The IVF process is not for the weary. Zac and I hired a babysitter and sat through needle-injection classes. We rearranged our life to schedule the shots, and when it was not convenient—Christmas dinner in Texas with my in-laws, during a movie, or my personal favorite, the back of an airplane while the flight attendant held a screaming Jordan—we improvised. Zac would lovingly apologize as he prepped the area and then stuck me with a needle. I knew his guilt was reemerging: that it was my body that had to go through all of this. I was the one who had to be at the doctor's office by 5 a.m. so I could be first in line to get my blood drawn and arrive at work before 7:30 a.m. I was the one who needed to do the injections alone while Jordan toddled around me if he couldn't come home from work. I was the one who inserted hormones into my body for the next two years. I also knew if he'd been able to, Zac would have taken all of that on himself. I just added the steps to my to-do list, put my head down, and did what I needed to do to have another child.

Our first attempt of hormone injections, egg extractions, and fertilization produced one viable embryo. We were hopeful but learned two weeks after the implementation that the pregnancy was not viable. The nurse practitioner called me to gently break the news five minutes before I had to lead my first professional development meeting at work. I had spent the previous years compartmentalizing; I swallowed this down as well and moved through my presentation.

We once again moved through the steps for our second attempt: hormone injections, egg extractions, fertilization. We learned it was possible to overnight mail hormone drugs during a vacation to rural Vermont—medical ingenuity was mind-blowing, and hope could take you a long way.

This time, we had two viable embryos.

We implanted them both.

My memory of the IVF process is just a patchwork. It wasn't because the medical procedures tested my limits, it was the severity of the stakes. I couldn't permit myself to be present, as if breathing too deeply would undo the entire process.

There is one clear memory, though. I am lying on an examination table in the corner room, with my arm above my head, as I squint into a screen. Then I listen to the doctor say: "Mr. and Mrs. Moore, congratulations. We have two heartbeats."

CHAPTER 17
Level of Pain
Tolerance—High

I spent the next nine months willing two tiny bodies to grow safely inside my own. I started acupuncture to help my body embrace this dramatic change. I stared at the ceiling and designed a nursery in my head while tiny needles stuck out of my body. It was, after all, the activity I chose most often when I needed to calm my body: organizing spaces. I was happy for a break from home. Jordan was in a potty-training phase where she did nothing but scream, she thought my expanding belly was a bouncy house, and I had to learn to teach high school while four little feet were interrupting my lessons. Any moment I could escape was priceless.

We had just completed our amniocentesis, which assured us the babies were perfectly healthy. We asked to learn the genders because we didn't want any more surprises: two boys. As the blue-haired waitress at the Jewish diner said to my stomach, "Boys, huh. You got a lot of *schmekels* in there." Sure did.

I tried to maintain a very low-key pregnant profile. This was a bit difficult when I lost the feeling in my right leg as I was trying to sit through doctors' appointments with a tantrummy Jordan, but I was managing to stay unusually calm. Yet when it all became a bit too much, I would beached-whale-style my way to my bed and imagine the lines of my bedroom ceiling as the layout of the babies' future room. Cribs, changing table, rocking chair. Chairs? Did we need two? Even when the technician found something worrisome on Baby A's brain, I was too distracted by Jordan's behavior to take in all the information.

"One of the babies might have something going on," I shared with Zac over dinner. I factually explained the impending MRI the technician had scheduled for me. Whether I was optimistic or delirious, it didn't matter: the baby would be fine.

Fine.

Weeks later, the twins and I shoved ourselves onto the patient table of the MRI to check it out. Jordan was in the middle of a new potty-training boot camp, the one where you don't leave the house, and Zac had his hands full with sticker charts. It was best to divide and conquer. I'd had an MRI before, so I was not nervous about the procedure. However, this time my stomach was so pronounced, it barely had any clearance, and my head was fully inside the machine. If I tilted my neck slightly, I could peek out the top and see the shadow of the exit sign. I felt completely trapped.

"If you are uncomfortable or need a break, pull on the cord and you can come out," the lackluster technician advised.

"Okay. I'm feeling like it's a bit hard to breathe in this position."

"Nah"—gum chomp—"you will be fine. What you got in there, triplets?"

"Just two."

The first two minutes of the anticipatory seventy-five I needed to spend in the machine were some of the hardest of my life. My low-key pregnant mode was long forgotten; I couldn't find my breath. I pulled weakly on the cord.

"I don't think I can do this," I gasped.

"Just keep going. You will be fine."

My ability for self-advocacy was dampened by the flimsy gown, the extreme fear, and the lack of oxygen. I weighed my choices.

1. Leave now only to return when my stomach is even bigger.

2. Lie on this table.

I cranked my neck to make out the rim of the exit sign, a symbol even too obvious for me. *Inhale.* Time to figure out the paint color for the nursery walls. *Exhale.* The twins have never heard the entire first act of *Les Misérables*, so I might as well serenade them now. *Inhale. I got you, boys,* and I began softly humming.

Upon the release from my torture chamber, I was wheeled into the fetal medical specialist's office to get my results. I extended my trembling right hand while my left was affixed firmly to my babies.

"I do not shake hands," the doctor declared without looking up from my paperwork.

I don't do well with people who aren't warm. I cried for a week when I was scolded in sixth-grade art class for talking out of turn. This would be especially ugly when I was in such a vulnerable state and hormonal. I swallowed my emotions and listened to the results.

"Well, it looks like Twin A has an excess of fluid in the brain. We are concerned about hydrocephalus. But I don't think he will be retarded."

Shit. I had spent so many lessons in my class advocating for my students to avoid the use of this word, and here I was sitting with the world's unfriendliest doctor, shaking, exhausted from retelling Victor Hugo's saga, and too depleted to be an advocate for anyone.

"If I could have my paperwork, please, I will be leaving. Thank you, Doctor."

I called Zac from the parking garage. He only heard fragments: excessive fluid, breathing, "Castle on a Cloud," blue paint.

"Just get home safely. I will take care of you," his warm voice reassured me. "Just get home safely." He knew that I, like Jordan, needed simple directives repeated while in an agitated state.

It was the same voice I needed the following week when he rushed me to the emergency room. I had woken up that morning, managed to put on my favorite maternity muumuu, only to be met with crippling pain on my right side.

Something was wrong.

The source of trauma couldn't be determined until the doctors could get twenty minutes of uninterrupted heartbeats from both babies. Up to this point, these precious children were too busy dancing in my belly to ever sit still for a strong checkup, so there was no way they were going to get this information while I was writhing in pain. I was unrecognizable, shouting profanities, and needed to be restrained in my hospital bed. My entire body was on fire. This was labor, spinal fluid headache, and blood patch pain combined.

The doctor firmly took my face in her hands. "I need you to do this for me. I need you to lie still for as long as you can. We need to make sure your babies are okay, and we have to act fast. You are the only one who can help me do this." She was assertive and squeezed my hand. "You can scream but you cannot move."

I wish I could say we moved on to Act Two of *Les Misérables* or figured out what shade of blue paint I wanted, but instead I closed my eyes, tapped into the last reserve of strength I had, cried out in pain, crunched on my husband's hand, and forced my body to not move.

The cause: a kidney stone.

Two bags of fluid later, the doctor peeked her head into my room.

"Hi." I smiled weakly at her.

"I was afraid to come in here," she joked.

"It's safe. Some would even say I'm sweet when my urinary tract isn't being sliced open."

"I can see that. We will get you home soon."

One sleepless night of *House Hunters* later, I had solidified Open Air blue as my wall color of choice and passed my kidney stone. No, thank you, I didn't want to keep it in the complimentary beaker like my fifth-grade teacher's show-and-tell trophy. I was ready to go home, take a warm shower, and await the birth of my twins.

Because after all of this, I imagined having two children consecutively wouldn't actually hurt at all.

CHAPTER 18
Seriously, Universe

The first time I saw my sons was in a photo.

After two years of IVF, thirty-seven weeks, and one day of growing babies, and twenty-three hours of labor, Baby A and Baby B made their appearances in the world. However, my doctor feared I would form blood clots, which meant I couldn't meet them right away.

I heard their cries just before they were whisked to the NICU. The nurses said they needed a little help breathing. I didn't blame them; I had been trying to figure it out for years.

Zac was able to meet them, and he took photos of their tiny, swaddled bodies. It was surreal looking at those children. They were not just cute babies, like the Anne Geddes art I used to hang on my walls in elementary school, they were *my* children.

Zac raced back to the recovery room to show me while a nurse was catapulting herself on my exhausted body to reduce any blood clots.

"We can name them when we see them in person," he said, squeezing my hand. This was a brave move as I had probably broken some of his fingers in labor.

Five hours of painful blood clot reducing gymnastics later, I was wheeled to the NICU.

I knew my sons immediately. I knew which little face was Austin Henry and which was Oliver Jacob. Zac and I didn't hesitate to determine which name suited which child. They didn't look anything alike, except squishy and perfect. There was nothing, not even oxygen masks, that would interrupt our joyful moment. I reached through the barrage of wires to hold their tiny hands.

"Welcome to the family, boys," I whispered. "Your sister Jordan is very excited to meet you."

"How wonderful," the nurse on duty smiled at as. "Your older daughter must be so excited to meet her twin brothers. You are so lucky to have a helpful older child."

"I'm not sure I would use the world *helpful*," I giggled. "But, yes, she is excited."

I settled into the chair in the NICU, snuggled between two tiny perfect humans. *Inhale.* It was time to let go of the 5:00 a.m. checkups at the fertility doctor, the midnight shots, and the false alarms. It was time to let go of the memory that the last time I'd held a newborn baby, I'd learned within hours of her birth that she would need surgery. It was time to let go of the fear. Our family was complete. *Exhale.*

"Well, Mr. and Mrs. Moore, the babies are making great progress. They will be off of their oxygen soon, and you should be home in a few days. We have determined Austin's fluid in the brain is more significant than we thought, so we want to help you get set up with a neurosurgeon consult. He will need an MRI." The doctor took time explaining the findings.

Just like that, new words added to the dictionary of words we never wanted to hear. *Cri du chat* meet *ventricle, shunt, corpus callosum.* (Didn't we go there on our Italian honeymoon?)

As the neonatologist turned the corner, I turned to my husband and asked, "What do you think it's like to have a baby and not be told you need a serious specialist within twelve hours? I mean, it must be nice, right?"

We were overwhelmed. Of course we were terrified. Brain surgery. My own brain furiously searched for my pep talk: *kindness for myself. Whatever thoughts I am feeling are valid. I am not made of robot parts.*

When that didn't work, I called Rachel. My sister was a constant source of calm for me. It didn't matter that she had two small children at home when I called at midnight to tell her about Austin's prognosis. She lovingly talked me through my next steps and reminded me there were some wins on this night. There was no spinal headache to distract me, and I didn't have to revisit my old friend Bessie the breast. My only job was to kiss her new nephews.

Delirium told me my family couldn't possibly have a child with a rare diagnosis and another who would need brain surgery. That seemed a bit excessive. Hope told me that everything would be fine. Anger said, *Seriously? I got a kindness award in high school—I don't deserve this shit.*

I wanted to focus on my tiny newborns, who had once only lived in my imagination. Instead, Zac and I called my uncle who was a neonatologist to get a recommendation for a neurosurgeon. He assured me he would be with me throughout every step. The nurses in the NICU scheduled our appointment for later in the week and helped me start to update our insurance. I was horrified to learn that within a week, my new baby would have to go into an MRI machine, and I would spend that day speaking with a doctor who performed brain surgery on babies.

With the support of the nurse, Austin was positioned safely against my chest and Oliver was snuggled into Zac. We rocked them in our designated chairs. I looked around the NICU, surrounded by tiny babies hooked up to machines and the families who were loving them to grow. It is a place for true warriors. I smiled at the mother ten feet from me, rocking her newborn. Behind her was a purple butterfly sticker. I didn't know what it meant then, but I noticed how beautiful it was.

"You have twins," she whispered.

"Yes. Two boys."

"We were supposed to have a boy and a girl. We lost her," she glanced at the butterfly sticker. She stopped speaking as her wife lovingly put an arm around her.

"I am so sorry." I didn't want to melt in front of this grieving mother, but I also couldn't escape the joy on her face looking at the baby in her arms. "Your baby, he's beautiful."

"Thank you. He is strong enough, so we are going home tomorrow."

I followed her lead. "That's wonderful."

We sat in silence, rocking our babies together. This is parenthood. A continual tug-of-war between sorrow and joy, trying to not let them split you apart as you tightrope-walk between them. It is as the poet Khalil Gibran explains, "[T]hey are inseparable. Together they come, and when one sits alone with you at your board, remember that the other is asleep upon your bed."

I fought to silence grief in this moment and searched for something to help me find the joy. I hummed Jacquie's favorite lullaby into Austin's ear. It would be one that soothed him for years to come. I willed the generations of families to once again wrap their hands around ours. We would be going home soon. I would introduce my sons to their incredible big sister, who had spent the day attempting to ride a tricycle with her grandparents, something that was never supposed to happen. We fought to go beyond expectations in this family; these boys would be no different. I had spent more time crying in the past four years of my life than I had in the previous three decades, so on the night my sons were born, I preferred to hum rather than sob.

CHAPTER 19
I Can Parallel Park Too

When the boys were released from the NICU, the nurse escorted us out of the hospital to head home. She gave me two pieces of advice: avoid heavy lifting and cover the car seats with a blanket, as strangers love to touch newborn twins.

As we waited for Zac to bring around our new minivan, suitable for a family of five, an elderly woman walked right up to me, took the lightweight blanket off Austin's carrier, and tried to pinch his cheeks. The nurse smiled. She had been at this job a long time. *I will take her advice*, I thought.

Which is why I felt extremely guilty when I found myself waddle-running down West 165th Street with a ten-pound car seat and a six-pound newborn baby. Zac and I were taking Austin for his MRI at the hospital; Oliver was with us because I was nursing them both. My mom had come over to watch Jordan and we left with plenty of time to get there, but the traffic on the Westside Highway was less than cooperative. I called the doctor's office, frantic, and the receptionist confirmed that if I missed the appointment, they did not have another opening until the end of the month.

Missing this appointment was not an option. "Let me out of the car; I'll run him there," I said to Zac.

"No."

"We have no choice. You can meet me with Oliver after you park the car, but we won't make it."

I made him pull over, and then I unlocked the door, grabbed a sleeping Austin, and off we went. When we arrived at the office, a sweaty, frantic mother and a doll-faced, sleeping baby, the receptionist told me I was on the wrong floor. I begged her to call ahead for me. She did one better, she escorted me to the correct floor and room herself.

This was not our first infant MRI; Jordan had received hers at age one, when we were determining the cause of her delays. For a newborn, they believed swaddling the baby after nursing would be enough to keep him still for the procedure. While Oliver and Zac waited outside the room, I carried Austin into the gigantic machine. My exhausted body leaned forward, and I held on to the bottom of his swaddle. The technician asked me to remove my glasses, and so I sat there unable to see, gripping the tiny toes of my newborn baby.

The neurosurgeon called two days later to make an appointment to review the scans. Austin would be thirteen days old when he met the neurosurgeon. Jordan had an important doctor's appointment on the same day, so Zac took her while I took the twins. The division of labor was easy; I was their food source. I was nervous to go to the doctor by myself. It was my first time driving the twins, and I was not super comfortable driving a minivan into Manhattan. This would usually be an event I would ask someone to come with me for; however, no one was available, so I had no choice but to pack up my diaper bag, check my rearview mirror, and ignore the honks from the other drivers.

When I arrived (with only three honks, thank you), the receptionist informed me that the doctor was a bit late because his surgery was running over. "No problem," I politely told her. We were safely parked and had nowhere to be. This man could take as long as he needed to operate on tiny brains. I was both in awe of this profession and shocked that I was there for him to meet my son.

We were escorted to a quiet office at the end of a long corridor. There were drawings, photos, and diplomas hanging on the wall.

"Austin," the doctor said as he came closer to examine the sleeping boys. "That's a great city. I'm from Texas. You know it is hard to get good barbecue up here."

"Yes, my husband is Texan. He says that all the time." I liked this man already.

He delicately measured Austin's head circumference. He examined the scans and determined Austin had moderate ventriculomegaly, meaning his ventricles did have excess fluid. By clinical standards, there was no evidence of hydrocephalus, a word I knew because it was the opposite of Jordan's tiny head concerns. He determined that Austin would need to be monitored for a year and we would return every two months to see him. If there were no changes, he would not require a shunt or any type of surgery.

I spent the remainder of the year continuing to receive good news from the doctor and decreasing my honk frequency. When he released us from his care a year later, Zac and I did a dance of joy around our double stroller. The doctor left us with three messages: surgery was not going to be needed, the excess fluid might cause learning delays, and please notify him if we ever found great barbecue in the area.

He set us up with future appointments: a strict schedule for a neurologist, an eye specialist, and a rheumatologist, with Early Intervention evaluations to follow.

Not a problem—it wasn't brain surgery.

CHAPTER 20
Twin Montage

My favorite part of any movie is the montage scene. I love watching the protagonist zoom through their challenges. A camera pans through changing seasons, and jogging girls complete a marathon. I remember wishing for a real-life montage when I got to college and attempted to study. Cue girl: staring at book, wiping brow, sipping tea, and the next day, graduating. I was rather disappointed to learn there was no splicing of scenes, and I had to actually read the information. It would have been far more glamorous to see six minutes of me pretending to read and then receiving my diploma.

My desire to live my life in a movie came true when I learned what it meant to nurse newborn twins. My brain was so on fire from exhaustion that I can only remember clips, and—ta-da—they were walking.

There was no delineation between day and night for me, but when Jordan was awake, the boys spent a lot of time rocking in their swings and practicing tummy time in a section where Jordan wouldn't use them as tiny ponies. We set up the portable crib for her, although at four she was far too big, so there was a safe place for her if we needed to do something for the boys. This just created a lot of equipment in the house. When it was time to "sleep," we placed two bassinets next to my side of the bed. By the time I'd finished nursing both and pumping so I could create bottles for Zac to help me, I had forty-five minutes to sleep before I did it again. I often spent a lot of my nursing time dropping granola bar crumbs on top of their heads and talking to the character Kristina Braverman from the television program *Parenthood*. She was really making a difference for her son.

"Zac." I nudged him awake. "I think we should start a school for Jordan like Kristina Braverman did. Her son has autism, and he is thriving there."

"Okay, honey."

I'm fairly sure I scribbled down on Austin and Oliver's food schedule: *Ask Kristina. Start school.*

"Wait, Zac."

"Huh," he said, and half rolled over.

"Also, look how cute her shirt is."

Delirious.

When the world thought it was morning, I would change into my other pair of oversized sweatpants, because a lady has to look presentable. I would pack the three kids up and drop Jordan off at her Early Intervention preschool. Someone from the school generously met me every morning, so I didn't have to schlep small babies into the building. On a good day, I would go home for some tummy time snuggles and mommy music class. On a bad day, I would drive to the Westchester mall to slug-walk past the fit, legging-wearing mommies power walking. They were always very gracious as they lapped me.

I'm sure some other things happened, but I'd have to ask Kristina Braverman to be sure.

CHAPTER 21
English Lesson 1—
A Metaphor

So here we are. Parents in the most unexpected way.

Round 1: a child with a rare genetic disorder

Round 2: twins (no brain surgery needed)

As the quote in the boys' bedroom reads, *Let the wild rumpus start!*

Many ask, "How do you manage? I can't imagine what your house must be like."

Due to the forty-five-minute sleep schedule, my brain is not capable of deep intellectual thought. So I rely on my trade, a metaphor for this crazy whirlwind: parenting is like a ride on the cheese bus.

My daughter acquired this phrase, "the cheese bus," from one of her favorite speech therapists, and the term just stuck. The school bus we were preparing for her to ride was yellow; so was cheese. Despite her excitement in talking about the bus, she was petrified of stepping onto it. Now that there were more nap schedules to accommodate in the house, though, it was an integral next step in achieving something that resembled balance.

Jordan, now four, had been studying the bus social story for seven months. We had several social stories in our home library: visiting the grocery store, driving in a car, using the potty—which was still a distant dream. Every single interaction, experience, or lesson that Jordan was accomplishing was a result of this direct instruction and preplanning.

We brainstormed a plan. Let the teachers manage the hard part. Jordan would only take the bus *home* from school: they could strap her in kicking and screaming, and we'd be the heroes to wait for her return.

Our fateful day had arrived. Zac was still at work and I was home on maternity leave. I received a call from her teacher. "She is on the bus. It took three of us to get her to settle, but she is in and on her way home. She will be there at three o'clock."

2:55 p.m.: I was a teenager waiting for the raging party to start. I had spent the last hour moving the portable crib of sleeping one-month-old babies in front of the window, straightening up the "Welcome Home, Jordan" sign, repositioning the store-bought cupcakes, and clutching the paperwork with the arrival information.

3:10 p.m.: It must just be a few minutes late. Our house doesn't have a clear number anyway.

3:30 p.m.: "I'm sorry, we have no information about that bus or its arrival at this time," the bus company operator stated.

3:40 p.m.: I decided to be outside to wave down the bus. I waddled (post-childbirth style) through the door with my mismatched shoes, oversized sweatpants, and unidentifiable smell. *Oh crap, the babies.*

3:45 p.m.: "The bus company handles all the timing," the school receptionist replied. "Call them."

3:46 p.m.: I stood in the middle of the street with one baby inside a carrier and the other propped awkwardly on top. I was dripping with every type of imaginable body fluid, looking inside every car. Maybe the bus had broken down and a stranger had taken her.

3:47 p.m.: My friend arrived to meet the babies for the first time. I threw her a kid. Third phone call: "I'm sorry, ma'am. We have no information at this time." I hung up because I could not even waste a moment yelling at the dispatcher—I needed to call the police.

3:50 p.m.: I was straight out of central casting for: disheveled, desperate, panic-stricken mother. I saw a bus. I staggered down the street, clutching a now wailing infant. "Excuse me. Do you have a curly-haired girl on that bus?!"

3:55 p.m.: The bus U-turned toward my driveway. A pink tutu appeared.

"Hi, Mama. Cheese bus. I hungry." She smiled.

I guided her slowly down the oversized steps with my one free hand and managed to squeak out to the bus driver, "I was very worried. You are incredibly late."

"We are sorry. It won't happen again."

I continued to mumble something as I stepped back from the bus. I know I should have said more. So many others in my position would have lit into this woman, but I didn't have the energy for more. I wanted to save whatever was remaining for the surprise party we had waiting for Jordan in the kitchen.

I was not sure I was going to be successfully able to parent three children. I had not planned for any of this, yet here I was. This was my life. These were my children. They deserved a mother who was not thrusting herself into oncoming traffic to search for them.

But this "cheese bus" adventure, this was parenting. You live through the frenzy, the fatigue, and the fear. Then comes momentary relief, reinvigoration, and rejoicing, just before you swing back around again.

During this moment, Jordan never saw my fear. She didn't know I was imagining a scene from *Law & Order* for a child who didn't have the language to get herself home. She never knew how helpless I'd felt or how unraveled I'd become in the forty-five minutes waiting for her. She didn't need to know. She just needed me to turn on the music for the dance party and hand her a celebratory cupcake.

During this time, none of my children would see my fear. Austin and Oliver were far too young to remember anything anyway, so I didn't have to worry about the long-lasting imprint of my concern. Austin would never know my fear as his head was measured routinely to see if the fluid had increased. He didn't know we were worried about his frequent eye crossing and the potential impact of the excess fluid.

He didn't need to know. He just needed me to be there at the end of every long day to rock him to sleep.

Oliver didn't know how worried I was that I couldn't find enough time in the day. While his brother and sister were being examined by doctors, he was left to stare at his reflection in the mirror. He didn't know how many times he was left with a babysitter while his parents sat throughout another taxing meeting. He didn't need to know. He just needed me to tickle him during tummy time and snuggle with his stuffed monkey, Bobo.

And that is what it feels like to be a special needs mother. A twin mother. A parent. We are often frightened, exhausted, lost, and waiting—but we manage the unexpected ride and find any excuse to bust into a dance party when it's done. What other choice do we have?

PART II
THE WILD RUMPUS STARTS

"If you suddenly and unexpectedly feel joy, don't hesitate. Give in to it ... Anyway, whatever it is, don't be afraid of its plenty. Joy is not made to be a crumb."
—MARY OLIVER

Parenthood: A Play

SETTING:
Any day. Doesn't matter. Could be 9 a.m. or 5 p.m.

CHARACTERS:
PARENT: Tired, hungry, needs to pee, late for something
CHILD: Screaming, full booger protruding from left nostril, blue paint on right eyebrow

PARENT: Hello, honey.
CHILD: [Inconsolable wailing]
PARENT: I'm sorry, but … (mark all that apply)

❏ You cannot go to school with only socks on your hands. You need pants.
❏ I will not wear a diaper on my head while I change you.
❏ I cannot reattach your decapitated ice pop.
❏ I don't have any more bandages for your imaginary cut. You already have twelve.
❏ The sky cannot be any bluer today.
❏ I can't make a fire truck appear right at this moment.
❏ Your eyeball did not fall into the toilet.
❏ I can't call an astronaut to bring your balloon back.
❏ I won't say "activate penis" every time you pee.

CHILD: [In a range only whales can decipher] But, Mommeee … .
PARENT: Fine, here is Mommy's phone to watch YouTube videos.
I have it cued to the random kid opening toy eggs.

[Aside] I heard he makes $3 million a year. Somehow, we are doing
this wrong.

[End of play]

CHAPTER 22
A Note to Beyoncé

Dear Beyoncé,

Congratulations on your twins. I, too, was pregnant with my twins after already having an older child. I also was balancing a full-time job. Some would say that reading one hundred ninth-grade papers on *Romeo and Juliet* is similar to performing at the Super Bowl, as they both require a lot of mental focus—so I don't have to tell you that you really need to take care of yourself and prioritize what you can during this time. Spending some quality time with your daughter will also really help her feel connected to you before her siblings come.

You will soon enter the Exhaustion Phase. The babies really suck out all the energy you have. Also, you have now basically tripled your hormones. Your alter ego is called Sasha Fierce. I call mine Patty. Mostly, she just wants cheeseburgers and will yell at you if you chew too loudly near her, but if you feed her Snickers bars, she seems to calm down just fine.

Also, it's really hard to get sleep during this phase because you are still chasing around your older child, but put your feet up when you can and just watch *Gilmore Girls* like the rest of us.

If you want to call me directly, Queen B, I can give you the gritty details. But here's the long and short of it—it is crazy to have two humans come out of you. Mine were thirty-four minutes apart and I got a lot of high fives and the promise of a pudding cup if I worked hard enough. I'm sure if you ask, they will give you one too.

Here is a script you should follow to answer every question in the first year.

1. Yes, they are twins.
2. No, they are not identical. Sure, that one could look more Jewish.
3. Good luck to your cousin's neighbor's babysitter's bus driver who also has twins.
4. Yes, I am nursing. No, I will not show you how I do it in tandem.
5. Why, yes, I do have my hands full.

So, Ms. Knowles, welcome to the multiples club. There is an organization for families of twins, did you know? If you have fifty dollars to spare, you can go to their annual picnic or clothing drive. It is an incredible adventure raising twins, and I wish you nothing but the best.

Oh, and my mom, Mona, came to stay with us for a month after they were born. If you need some extra help, I'm sure you could call her; she makes great slow-cooker dishes.

P.S. I have discovered that any time you forget to do something, you get a free pass when you say, "I am so sorry. I just had twins." No one will know if they are college age. They will always say, "Wow, no problem. We understand."

Try it. It works.

CHAPTER 23
Salami at the JCC

I have a secret. We brought salami to the Jewish Community Center. Well, just the parking lot.

It was a necessity.

Let's create some context. I am Jewish. My husband is not. I don't eat pork. My husband loves bacon. His original plan for our theoretical children was to have "Christian Days" to determine when they were permitted to consume pork products. I thought it might be confusing. Enter imaginary child. *Mommy, how come Cynthia is eating prosciutto on Monday? I thought Tuesday was the day we ate ham.* So we decided that, for clarity, our future children, whenever we had them, would not eat pork.

Then we had actual children. And we soon learned that whatever they will eat is good enough. That means if salami is the only thing they will put in their body, they can have salami. For now. Your Jewish mother will proudly ask for it at the deli counter—thick slices, please. We choose our battles.

This trick became helpful when Jordan started a dance class. The Jewish Community Center, the JCC, was the only place in our area that would accommodate Jordan's needs. She had been demonstrating a passionate interest in music and movement from her early days of giggle and roll, so we wanted to find a place where she could express herself freely. Despite their rigorous program, the JCC understood that Jordan just desired a place to move, regardless of if she was still in a diaper, wearing the wrong footwear, and avoiding the formation. Ballet Friday was her favorite day of the week, and we were going to do everything we could to make it happen.

Despite our enthusiasm, this was going to be complicated for a few reasons.

Reason A: a mother's stubbornness

I decided I could venture to the JCC with all three of my kids. I was desperate for some alone time with my children. I was so grateful for all the support; however, I rarely got to parent independently. Besides, I wanted to learn what some traditional experiences were like, such as attending dance class. I ignored all the suggestions for help and resolved that this was, in fact, our best plan.

Reason B: sensory integration disorder

The fancy explanation for this is that the brain is unable to respond to the information from the body's sensory system. But in simple terms, Jordan fatigued quickly. It took a lot of energy for her to process the world. We had just learned the concept of spoon theory, coined by Christine Miserandino, which explained that every individual maintains a theoretical number of spoons on a given day. Each task completed is a different number of spoons. In my interpretation, it looked like:

Folding laundry: 1

Assembling anything from IKEA: 14

While a typical person can regenerate their spoons each day, an individual with an illness or a disability only has a fixed amount. While I might use one-quarter of a spoon to get ready in the morning, that event for Jordan might use up one entire spoon. Every decision, movement, and action throughout the day uses up your spoons, or energy, and when they are gone, a breakdown will occur. Her body was not always able to accommodate her interest to dance, so all we could do was try.

These challenges created a basic formula for disaster: my child would most likely reach her breaking point at this time of day + my hands were too full to help her = need for special elixir to keep her moving (aka: plastic container of cold cuts).

Situation A: It was January. Snowing. I couldn't get her coat over her defiant shoulders, so I settled for pink winter boots and mismatched gloves. She had consequently removed these items in the car, and while her occupational therapist would be impressed, she was left with her flimsy ballet skirt and short-sleeved shirt. No shoes. I pushed five-month-old twins in the double stroller while simultaneously carrying my forty-pound daughter on the handlebars. I carried her dance bag, my diaper bag, her coat on my left shoulder, and when her dance bag fell, I kicked it soccer style through the parking lot. Cristiano Ronaldo would be proud.

Situation B: February. The twins were a robust twenty-five pounds each and I carried them and their fifteen-pound car seats up a flight of stairs, leaving the double stroller at the bottom. If there were an elevator in this building, I had not found it yet. I called to Jordan to remain at the bottom of the stairs until I came to get her, as she was not ready to navigate them independently. I held a dance bag, a diaper bag, a bottle bag, my purse, and the extra diapers we wanted to donate. I left the babies at the top of the stairs, returned down the stairs to get her, carried her up the stairs, and repeated this process for two more floors. It's like dance class came with a free gym membership.

Situation C: March. I changed three sets of diapers while the dressing room filled with school-age ballerinas. I deflected questions about why Jordan was still wearing a diaper when she was so big. Jordan insisted on wearing the dance skirt on her head. Austin and Oliver crawled in opposite directions, Hungry, Hungry Hippos style.

At the end of every class, we repeated the stairs process and returned to the safety of our car. My favorite time of day is still when they are all latched in their car seats and we just sit. No one can get into any trouble locked behind those harnesses.

Long after my maternity leave ended, I continued this late-afternoon adventure. Four semesters of dance class, and only a few people ever offered to help. Most commented, "Wow, you have your hands full," and "I feel tired just watching you."

Perhaps there was an assumption that I had this under control. I was also trying to convince myself I didn't need any assistance. I was too stubborn to ask someone for help or even hire a babysitter to come along. Although I truly needed it, until I learned to ask for it, I relied on my secret weapon: salami.

I'm so sorry, JCC—it is a necessity that there will be pork products near the premises. At least until I learn how to stand up for myself. But just in the parking lot.

We promise.

CHAPTER 24
BaBa

I returned to work when the twins were one and Jordan was five. We needed to restart our search to find someone who could manage the needs and chaos of our home. We questioned, once again, if it were better for one of us to stay home with the children, but we quickly recognized, once again, that we were better suited in the classroom teaching other people's children. We needed to remain parents to our children; we were the only people who could do that for them. Furthermore, Zac and I loved being teachers, and with our chaotic life, we deserved a sliver of personal success. So LaLa introduced us to one of her family members, BaBa. When you have kids with speech issues, you say whatever names you can.

Barbara, as the adults called her, was our new, incredibly tranquil babysitter, and she had lovingly taken on the mayhem of our house. It was quite the house. By the time we completed our tenth activity of the day, it was only eight a.m. I had once received a phone call from an appliance company to tell me that the receptionist had spent about five minutes on the phone with my giggling babies, who had somehow managed to hit redial and babble into the receiver. She loved it, but just wanted to make sure they weren't home alone. We were that family. A loving, chaotic mess. We couldn't find just anyone for the job.

Barbara was magical. In addition to managing Jordan's intensive schedule, mood swings, and quick costume changes, there were two infant boys and two very overscheduled working parents. Barbara would waltz into our kitchen before seven o'clock with a cheery "Good morning," despite the fact that I had again misplaced my keys, sat on a half-eaten banana, and was removing a crying Austin off my shin.

She was the calmest person I had ever met.

On her first day, a Spider-Man in training-sized Oliver propelled himself out of his crib onto his head. She picked him up and dusted him off, lulled him back to sleep, and didn't quit. She was not deterred by the natural chaos that emerged in a house of young children. It took a special person not to mind Jordan running around with a decapitated doll head as a ponytail holder. Barbara was a mother herself, after all. We knew our children were safe in her capable hands.

A month later, she was locked in our four-by-four bathroom for three hours, with only a toilet, a sink, and a copy of *Potty Time with Elmo*. The door handle on our old house would not budge, and Oliver and Jordan were especially unhelpful on the other side. Apparently, they thought seeing her fingers peep out the bottom and hearing her voice call to them was a silly game. They ran around the room watching *Descendants* from Disney on a loop and eating Goldfish cracker crumbs they found in the couch. When Zac got home, he saw two children with the world's droopiest diapers, then heard a gentle knock and a polite, "I am stuck in here."

I was not home for this adventure, because I was with Austin for his most recent doctor's appointment on the new saga, *What's going on with Austin?* His Early Intervention team was completely alarmed by Austin's progress. He had delayed gross motor skills, an unsteady gait, and proprioceptive issues, and he did not like vestibular input. Basically, he was floppy, dizzy, and wanted to remain in a reclining position. Zac and I sat in meeting after meeting with expert therapists who were certain there was a deeper diagnosis to find. We had been here before, so we followed up with each suggestion. The list of doctors in my cell phone was now officially longer than the number of friends I had.

Meanwhile, there were still two other children and full-time jobs to attend to. My mother had retired after Jordan's diagnosis to provide an extra set of hands for the schedules we needed to maintain, but her background in counseling was best suited for managing my fluctuating emotions. We needed Barbara to fill in for the moments that Zac and I could not manage. With these medical specialists, you do not get the luxury of scheduling an appointment after you've finished work and your child has properly napped. You take what you can get, arrange coverage, pack a bag of toys and snacks, and pray your children will nap in the car. With our support team in place—BaBa and Grandma—we were ready for round two of developmental delays.

We started the process again. We met our new therapists and scheduled a collaborative meeting. BaBa took over where LaLa left off, reposting new picture schedules to organize Austin's therapies and creating activities for Oliver to be entertained in a separate room. She coaxed Jordan, now in kindergarten, to use the potty while transitioning her for her afternoon therapies. Every day when I came home from work, I found my children clean, calm, and composed. I have no idea how she managed this. Three minutes home alone with me and the twins eat cereal off the floor like birds and Jordan paints her face with eye shadow to look like a coal miner.

When it was determined Austin would require strabismus surgery to correct his very adorable, and very pronounced, crossed eyes, it was Barbara who entertained Jordan and Oliver. When I was overwhelmed about putting eye drops in his bloodshot eyes, she calmly steadied my hand to show me how. When I was told by a physiatrist that Austin would have to wear orthotics and a tool they call hip twisters—tight chords that wrapped up and down his legs—to walk, on the very same day the rheumatologist told us Austin was not allowed to wear anything tight on his skin for fear of cutting off his circulation, it was Barbara who helped me advocate for him. When Jordan's bus arrived to take her to school, and Austin's bus arrived to take him to the same developmental day-care program, Barbara helped Oliver make a sign for his own bus—the family car—so he would also be included.

We knew Austin would be all right, because our barometer for parenthood was happy and healthy. He was both. We knew he would not need brain surgery and that he was experiencing developmental delays. With the support of Early Intervention, we found a nursery school that used direct instruction, which complemented his learning needs. He thrived. He did not have a diagnosis and might never receive one, but he was learning. We assumed the learning disabilities we were facing were a result of the excess fluid in his brain, but even now, we will never be sure. He was making progress; he just needed more support to get there. So did we.

We are fortunate to have found someone to support our family while we are at work. It helps to balance the weight. Zac and I are grateful to our extended village that can tranquilly float above tumultuous waters. It inspires us to do the same.

CHAPTER 25
It's a Date

Our marriage deserves a bit of attention, so we are continuously learning how to pamper it, as much as one can with three interrupting humans. Where we had previously spent our time climbing the ruins in Athens and strolling along the Thames, we were now getting boxed desserts from Whole Foods and waiting together in the ophthalmologist's office to see if our son had cortical visual impairment, temporary or permanent eye issues connected to the occipital lobe. Romance.

We had waited two months to get an appointment with this specialist. Despite Austin's recent strabismus surgery, there were still some serious concerns. Zac and I determined we could take a half-day, spend some quality time with Austin, and make an afternoon of it.

When we arrived at 1:00 p.m., the nurses had just ordered pizza for the waiting room, because, yes, it was going to take that long.

We played games with Austin. We read books. We ran up and down the hallway. We made friends with other tired parents and their overtired children. After two hours, our names were finally called. I let out a gleeful cheer while we quickly gathered our items: coats, hats, bags, open milk, half an apple, and—oops, Austin. We turned the corner and the nurse let us into the room. It was a second waiting room.

Romance.

"Plan to be here for a while." An exhausted dad on the floor sighed. He had been waiting for an hour already in this hotbox.

We sat there for another hour. Shoeless and practically engaged to the father on my right, I started to wilt. The soggy ophthalmologist pizza was not going to cut it. Zac caught my eye, reached over Austin's head, and put his hand on my back. He pretended like he was winding a key and winked. He pulled his hand away to reclaim his car keys from Austin's drooling lips.

This was our code. It started the day we got caught in the rain on the steps of Montmartre, backpacking in Paris. We were in our mid-twenties, carefree, and exploring some art before returning to our study abroad program in Dublin. We were in the middle of ascending the stairs when the rain hit, and I couldn't move my gigantic pack one more inch. He placed his hand on my back and wound an imaginary clock to propel me further.

Sometimes you forget as a couple that you have these idiosyncrasies. You forget you were ever someone carefree when you are now relinquished to a carpet square in a waiting room. Sometimes a small gesture to recharge you is all it takes.

Our names were called. Four hours from when we had arrived at the office. We gathered our items—coat, hats, bag, someone's shoe—and we entered the specialist's office.

He spent one minute looking at the baby and four minutes talking about his recent philanthropic work in Africa. "Well, thanks for coming," he said without opening Austin's chart. "He's fine."

Romance.

CHAPTER 26
The Making of a Memory

Once a month, a gigantic box of goodies would arrive on our front step, courtesy of Aunt Amanda. While we flew to Dallas every Christmas and summer, my sister-in-law was not able to fly to visit us. Flights were expensive from Texas, and she'd recently had a leg amputated, making traveling difficult. Even though she was struggling with her health, it did not stop Amanda from sending her love in a box to her niece and nephews in New York.

Jordan would climb into the box as if Aunt Amanda were hiding inside it. The boys would crawl around the outside of the box, mouthing the presents Jordan tossed their way. The items had usually been found at the local American Legion garage sale—she wasn't discerning. They ranged from erasers to bouncy balls, anything trivial. The only qualification seemed to be that the first time they looked at the item, it was the most wonderful thing they had ever seen, and after three intense minutes, they would never look at it again. Amanda's favorite were the oversized stuffed animals that had lost their stuffing. Sometimes she sent army knives or glass bottles. She just bestowed gifts, despite her lack of income and awareness of what was dangerous for small children, because she loved her family.

The practice of sending care packages was something Jacquie would have done, so Aunt Amanda filled those shoes. She made sure the kids knew just how passionately they were loved, even if she couldn't see them every day. Amanda often said that because she would probably never have children, she was thrilled to dote on Jordan, Austin, and Oliver like they were her own.

There were always notes inside for us, too, addressed to "baby." Everyone she met was "baby," especially older gentlemen at the grocery store who rode on scooters—one of her weaknesses. We would sift through notes commenting about the upcoming Cowboys game for Zac, or a book of sign language for me with a Post-it sticky note attached. *People told me I wouldn't talk either, but look at me now. Maybe this will help Jordan.*

While she didn't talk about her own developmental struggles often, Amanda's pep talks were endearing and gave me hope for the future. Amanda's prognosis had been more optimistic, yet there were many similarities with her niece. Jordan shared her aunt's panache for pink and people. They both were a little stubborn and loved fiercely. Amanda's cognitive and physical limitations had meant she was dependent on her parents and Zac for a lot of her needs, especially during their childhood, but it did not stop her from talking to her baby brother like the big sister she was.

"Zac, are you giving Jordan enough vegetables? I saw a lot of carrots at Costco."

"Yes, Amanda."

I imagined this was the same voice he used when she interrupted him playing video games as a teenager.

"Are the boys getting enough sleep? Did you tell them my Super Chick bedtime story yet?"

"Not yet, Amanda."

This favorite story was not quite ready to be a bedtime story for my infants, but it was a family favorite. When she and Zac were children, they would visit their grandparents' farm in Missouri. Amanda's favorite chicken, Super Chick, had been missing one day. When she questioned the family about it at dinner, the adults exchanged nervous glances before her granddad finally confessed, "Well, Amanda, we are eating Super Chick for dinner."

There was a very long pause and nervous tension before Amanda spoke again. "Well," she said, "tomorrow can we eat the cat?"

Zac giggled. "I'll tell them in a few years. We don't want them getting any ideas."

I loved observing the interaction between them. It was a little preview into what life in Houston in the eighties must have been like. Also, it was the closest look I had to seeing the dynamics between a child with special needs and a neurotypical sibling. This same protective gene was already present in Jordan as she would make sure the boys had their stroller blanket or favorite toy. It was a quality I hoped Amanda would continue to cultivate in Jordan.

"Let's call Aunt Amanda to thank her for the toys," Zac said to the kids.

Most of Amanda's phone calls would be filled with an exchange of noises between Jordan and her aunt while the twins gnawed on the phone. Amanda would sit on the other end, dipping her pickles in ketchup and telling us how her recent doctor knew nothing about her ailments. We were grateful for these quiet moments because we were often concerned that her next phone call would reveal she was in the hospital or needed another procedure. She would then explain to Zac her latest issues with her cell phone plan and the recent news she'd overheard on her police scanner.

"Can't wait to see you guys for Christmas. I always look forward to my all-you-can-eat shrimp date with my favorite little brother. Put my Jordie on; I want to say goodbye." She concluded every phone call the same way: "Jordie bug. Your aunt Mandy loves you big. You are going to do everything they said you wouldn't. I know you will. I love you big."

Jordan would put her arms wide out in front of her. Her sign for "Big."

As she got older, she would echo, "Love big."

Zac and I wanted a way for the kids to be connected to their loving aunt, beyond the box of toys and the annual holiday trip where she would just hold them and kiss them until they escaped her loving clutches. We added Amanda's effusive love into their nighttime routine. After we read the story, sang a song, and kissed them on their *keppies*, we whispered, "I love you big," before leaving the room.

It was as if Amanda's soothing, Southern voice were filling their rooms, even if she was far away. A reminder of what "love you big," and loving, was all about.

CHAPTER 27
Mom Brain

The effects of stress are not lost on me. My hair started to gray, I developed migraines, and my dentist commented on how impressive it was that I had cracked my indestructible mouth guard. The most dangerous impact has been my perpetual mom brain. "Mom brain" is best summed up by the card my sister sent me for my birthday two months after having her third child.

Dear Rachel (her name, not mine), *Happy Birthday. Love, Rachel*

Pregnancy brain is the universal connector of parenthood. We cannot recall words. You find yourself watching *Peppa Pig* even though there are no children in the room. You almost mistake your nail polish remover for mouthwash. You suggest Lane, the fictional character from *Gilmore Girls*, as a babysitter, because she is also familiar with the needs of twins. No one tells you how long the haze will last.

Around the twins' first birthday, I was driving the kids to physical therapy for Austin and Jordan. I had managed a small miracle to get their appointments scheduled back-to-back. A special needs mommy win. On this day, Austin had a gigantic blowout in his diaper, and I'd forgotten the diaper bag. It happens to the best of us. I was happy I'd remembered all three kids. Inside the therapy office, I stripped him down, rolls proudly on display, and wiped him with a napkin. While

I might have once felt shame, now I just paraded out of the bathroom with one very nude, very giggly baby boy. Another mother took pity on me and threw me her set of wipes, a diaper, and her backup clothes: a onesie with a portly bear holding up an Italian flag.

"It's his favorite. Can you bring it back next week?" she said kindly.

"Of course. Thank you so much."

Naturally, I forgot. I had remembered to wash it but hadn't put it in the dryer. I was resourceful and attached it to my window, letting it fly freely down the Bronx River Parkway. It did have a flag on it, after all.

In all this chaos, I had placed the keys on the top of the car so I had both hands to attach the shirt. My Jetsons-inspired car doesn't need the keys in the ignition; they just had to be in the vehicle—correction, *on* the vehicle—to work. About three exits later, something breezed past the onesie and my rearview mirror.

"Wouldn't that be terrible if those were my keys?" I chuckled. I loved talking to a car full of children who rarely talked back.

"Keys make car go," Jordan proudly declared.

"Very good, honey. Shit. Those were my keys."

"Shit," Jordan proudly stated.

My daughter swearing was going to be the least of my worries today. We had just finished hanging up artwork with each child's first word: Jordan (*Mama*), Austin (*up*), Oliver (*outside*). At least I didn't have to write out "shit" in colorful fingerpaints. Time to evaluate choices. If we didn't turn off the car, we would be fine. This meant we skipped physical therapy and Freddy would have to wait for his onesie; or I could get the spare key, be late for physical therapy, and throw off the very structured schedule of my oldest child. I drove to Zac's school, and called him three times before he picked up (in the middle of his theater class).

"Walk outside with the spare key. Mine are on the Bronx River Parkway."

I must be a delight to be married to; I don't even say hello anymore.

When I discovered later that I'd have to hand over two hundred dollars to replace the key, I was outraged. I also needed some semblance of control, even if it was over my technology, so that night I announced my plan. "I am just going to find the keys myself. I think I know where they fell." Delirium makes you very assertive.

I'd spend the next week driving fifteen miles per hour, at odd hours, with the hope of seeing my keys. At exit fourteen, lying on the side of the road, there they were waiting for me.

There was enough of a shoulder that I could double-park, put on my hazards, and run lovingly toward my pink carabiner and tire-marked *you are my jam* key chain. To my calculations and sense of smell, it appeared they'd survived one rainstorm and a visit from a flock of geese.

Sometimes sleep deprivation is dangerous. Sometimes it just makes you resourceful.

CHAPTER 28
Nothing Is Open on Sunday

A successful activity with all three children typically lasts seven minutes. When you break this down for an entire day in the house, it means we only need about fifty-one activities to get to nap time if nap time happens. We usually break up our days with a therapy session, a car ride, or the occasional visit; however, some days this cannot happen. Maybe there's a snowstorm, everyone has a fever, or the playground feels too daunting, but every parent has the inevitable day where there is nothing to do.

I attempt to start these days positively. *Today your only job is to enjoy being with your children. There is nothing else to get done. Just be present and enjoy.* In fact, it is rare for our family. Because we are always navigating so many appointments, it is rarely just the five of us. The boys had started walking and were adorably toddling around the house. On days like this, we didn't have to be a special needs family worried about progress; we could just be a family.

The monitor tells me at 5:00 a.m. that Jordan is ready to start her day. I place one foot on the floor, careful to avoid the avalanche of unfolded clothes. I imagine my hair is more Jackie O than Medusa, like those mothers in commercials, primped and ready to start the day. Jordan and I take our position, snuggled in front of the couch.

I have every intention of reading to her, but I can just doze during *Mickey Mouse Clubhouse* viewing number one, as I'm sure I can catch up with the Valentine's Day surprise for Minnie later in the day. By six o'clock, all three of the children, delicious in footy pajamas, are ready to complain about our breakfast options.

After teatime with stuffed animals, parachute play, and drumming in the kitchen cabinets, I call to Zac, "I think it's probably time to get their lunch together."

"It's only 8:20 a.m.," he laughs.

No problem. I am Zen Mom. I take a deep breath. I have nowhere to be. There is no rush. We snuggle on the couch watching *Mickey Mouse*, viewing number two: Mickey needs glitter to add to Minnie's valentine. Nice touch.

Fourteen activities into our day, we have had three tantrums, spilled four cups of milk, and gotten one accidental black eye from the piano bench; it is only 1:30 p.m. There is only so much Laurie Berkner dance party, block building, clay making, baby doll throwing that we can handle. We have landed on "music class with Mommy." If I must sing the dog barking verse of "Old MacDonald" for ten consecutive minutes, I will—because every moment is a precious opportunity to spend with my beautiful children. I will not dare to interrupt this activity if it is working, even if it is to identify what the large puddle is on the couch.

On a day like today, you can never really take too many baths. You ate some guacamole? Let's jump into the bath to wash that off. You had an ice pop at 9:00 a.m. and it's now in your hair? How about some bubbles to help rinse it away? You sat in that unrecognizable liquid on the couch—just a little soak. Each of those baths could be at least seven minutes, and we can continue ticking away at our activities.

We eat whenever and whatever we can. You found grapes on the floor—lunch! Just have to slice and peel them first. That takes a few extra minutes. Communal bag of chips while we watch *Mickey Mouse*, viewing number three: so the conflict is that Donald forgot Daisy's valentine—ah, plot twist. You will burn off those calories picking up the same set of LEGO blocks ten times anyway, so it all works itself out. For an added challenge, try to manage cleanup without twisting an ankle on the Hot Wheels cars.

Finally, it is bedtime. Well, it's close enough. They can't read the clock. Parental conveyer belt begins: rinse, wash, dry, brush, repeat. Repeat. Repeat. Repeat. The next time we have an entire day at home, we should just start at bedtime. It is never ending. We finally have them snuggled in their recently wiped-down pajamas (guacamole doesn't stain, and I never did finish that laundry). Then the quiet of the evening begins.

First stop, vacuum the cereal from the 10:00–10:06 a.m. game, Throw Cereal at My Brother. Zac loads and unloads the dishwasher with what appears to be only lids of sippy cups. I pick up doll heads and walk around in two circles before I realize I have no idea where these came from or where they belong. Although most of my evenings are spent daydreaming about what closet to organize next, I officially give up, throw any remaining items away, and go to check on the kids.

My children fall asleep in positions that match their personalities by day. Austin is cuddled with several items he was examining before he passed out, and is making a soothing puckering sound with his lips. In the crib next to his, Oliver lies with his legs and body flailed out around him, as if he fell asleep mid-thought. He has a small smile on his face as I kiss him good night. Across the hall, Jordan lies on her side with her arm above her head. When I try to remove her hat, she immediately jerks awake to grab it and reposition it on her head.

Before choosing which Netflix show we will escape into, Zac and I recap our favorite moments of the day. We spent so much time with them, we didn't even notice how wonderful they were. In a day of keeping them safe, kissing their boo-boos, and remembering their favorite foods, I missed so much. Doctor Oliver and his plastic stethoscope examining my ankle that was in fact injured on a Hot Wheels Lamborghini. Superhero Austin wearing a cape and bunny ears, dancing to a Raffi tape he discovered on an old boom box. Jordan, setting up an imaginary store to sell her Squishies, before throwing them into the air like confetti. There was also the one moment, when all five members of the house were together, looking at the pictures of a book. It was fleeting, but it happened. The successful parents send an air high five, too tired to actually move to get close to each other. Another long day completed. We all survived—well, except the couch. I really have no idea what that liquid is.

CHAPTER 29
Yes, My Hands Are Full

My turning point occurred the day a man yelled at me from his car. They are words I will never forget.

He must have seen us while we were shopping inside the store.

It was the first time we were going in without a stroller, and I knew chaos was sure to follow. I looked at six innocent eyes and reminded them, "Everybody do good listening for Mama, okay?"

We created the cutest chain of hand-holding I have ever been associated with. I was holding the hand of my oldest. She was now almost six, sporting a pink ball gown that she thought Pnina Tornai had designed, as a result of too many viewings of *Say Yes to the Dress*, but had really been on sale at Costco. Her red cowboy boots complemented her rainbow wig. She was holding hands with the twin tornados—Oliver, who refused to leave the house without a bright green arm warmer and his sister's hat, and Austin, covered in a mixture of guacamole and applesauce. It took us about ten minutes to get through the revolving door, but we had this.

We were here for a mission. We had not only graduated from the possibility of Jordan never speaking, but we were moving toward functional life skills. She had proudly remembered the four things we needed to buy. It was just a plus that her almost-two-year-old brothers were going with her. Jordan had spent all week working on identifying the items and was here to generalize the skill in the grocery store. With the support of her therapists, we had a modified PECS (Picture Exchange Communication System) where she could look at a picture of the item, and put it in her grocery cart. Today's haul included: strawberries, milk, ice pops, chocolate chip muffins.

This was one of those moments that special needs parents talk about. When they get a chance to take in a sip of success and focus on what is working. I was present and ready to take on this adventure with my three overeager children.

Aisle #1: "Looks like you have your hands full" greeted us in produce.

"Yes, it's our first time without the stroller," I heard my chipper voice respond.

"Strawberries!" My daughter spotted item number one. Off the three of them went.

Despite the fact that two of these children wore orthotics, and one wasn't supposed to even walk, they were suddenly faster than I could ever imagine. Their physical therapists would have been so proud.

Someone needs to tell the produce people that the height of the fruit is exactly wrong for almost two-year-old twins. They had each put five cartons of blueberries into the shopping cart, but they were not tall enough to drop them gently, so there was now an avalanche of tiny spherical berries surrounding the cart. Oliver sat on the floor to start eating them. "Yum, berries." Austin couldn't stop giggling, and our fearless leader was shouting, "Not on the list! Only strawberries!"

Aisle #2: I bribed Austin to sit in the front of the shopping cart with the stolen remnants of the berries I couldn't return to the package. This is a gentle reminder for consumers to wash your fruit before you eat it. Oliver was holding my hand and singing, and we were stopped by a fellow shopper at the deli counter. He astutely stated, "Looks like you have your hands full. I have two children. One is a newborn. I don't think I will ever take them to the grocery store."

I wanted to smile, because that is polite, but realized that instead of my three boisterous children, there were only two. Jordan was no longer next to me. "Would you excuse me? I seem to be missing one of them."

He backed away from me as I threw one kid into the back of the shopping cart while the other grabbed my glasses. "Nose."

"Yes, honey, that is Mommy's nose. Jordan! Can you hear me? Has anyone seen a little girl in a pink dress and a wig? There can't be many in the store."

I frantically flung myself past the soup aisle. No Jordan.

"Jordan, Mommy can't see you!"

And there it was—the pit I feel every day in my stomach had exploded. My worst fear: my child was missing. She didn't have enough language to ask for help. She hadn't learned yet to point to her shoe where we'd placed the sticker that had her name and my phone number. This was what happened when I allowed myself to celebrate a moment: I lost one of them.

This entire inner tirade was no longer than fifteen seconds, when I finally saw her in the snack aisle, examining a bag of pretzels.

"Hi, Mommy. Not on the list. Keep going."

There was no time for emotions to process. I would swallow that down for another day. I needed to get us through this store safely.

Aisle #3: I bribed Oliver with a lollipop to sit in the grocery cart as Austin insisted on pushing the cart while I carried him. My daughter was leading us toward the milk aisle. We walked past a maintenance worker and his full ass crack as he bent over the lobster tank.

"Look, Mommy, tushy."

"Yes, honey, I see it—let's move ahead."

I grabbed the milk with my other arm, threw it into the cart, and headed toward item number three.

Aisle #4: Everyone was now sitting inside the cart, squished blueberries on their pants, devouring the box of ice pops we'd just located. I returned to get a second box. Of course I left the wipes in the car.

An elderly woman with a cart full of avocados and cantaloupe approached us. "Well, you sure have—"

"My hands full, yes."

As we approached the final aisle, I complimented my daughter on her strong shopping skills. This was a big deal for her, and we had to finish the entire task to make the lesson stick. She was the most excited for item number four. The chocolate chip muffins. I, too, have never been more excited to purchase an item, because it meant we could go home.

We turned the corner and I could see, like a glaring spotlight: they were sold out.

"What about blueberry muffins? They are delicious."

"No! The list says chocolate chip!"

If you have ever been around a child, let alone one with special needs, the space between the expectation and the reality is frankly … painful. I was ready to handle the breakdown. I had my contingency plan in place. I wasn't *too* far from the beer aisle.

"Mommy." She took a deep inhale. "No muffins. Let's go home. My list done."

This momentous occasion practically made me float out of the grocery store. And for the record, not only did we not float, but we disrupted an entire display of candy bars, Oliver signed the credit card receipt, and my daughter did her best rendition of Ariana Grande's song "Side to Side." (Less than appropriate, but that's for another day.)

We piled into the car. A full fifty minutes after we had arrived. Four items in our bag. As I buckled the last car seat, I heard a man's voice shout from behind his steering wheel.

"Hey, lady."

"Yes."

"Hey. I saw you in there."

"Oh, I'm so sorry." I turn around, red-faced. "It was our first time—"

"You are a terrific mother. Have a great day."

Thank you, kind stranger. I will have a great day. A great day that will end with me trying to figure out how to turn strawberries, milk, and ice pops into a meal—because while we were at the grocery store, I didn't have any time to get dinner.

CHAPTER 30
The IEP Iceberg

There are 20.9 million families in the United States with one family member with a disability. Each of these families has had to navigate a difficult and exhausting process to make sure their child received the necessary services. There are inequities in this system. There is work to be done. This work becomes more challenging when it is compounded by cultural capital, the factors that shape how much power and voice someone has in the room. I am aware my upbringing, skin color, education, and profession enable me to navigate my circumstances with more ease. It wasn't until I became a teacher that I realized this was not the case for every family, which in itself is a sign of my privilege. The educational system of the United States, the system I spent my life learning from and giving back to, is flawed. We need to address these deficiencies, to change them.

When Jordan received her diagnosis, I knew it would be challenging to navigate the system, but I would find the support to do so. I am also aware that I have privilege to be heard in most of these spaces. When we attended our first conference for cri du chat, we met children with the same delays as Jordan receiving different levels of support through Early Intervention, a federal- and state-mandated program. There was one child whose state provided only three hours of therapy per week and who spent the remainder of the time in front of a television. Jordan received over twenty hours a week in New York. When the child ages out of Early Intervention, the discrepancies become larger. Each school district handles special education differently. We met a little boy in Atlanta who was in a self-contained classroom with one other child, and a girl in California who was fully integrated into a co-taught classroom and even received a part in the school play. Because each district had a different allocation of funds, the availability for each child differed.

Navigating the system is tricky, especially if you didn't major in educational or legal jargon. I can best explain it using the educational tool, the iceberg. It is a strong visual to help students understand what is going on below the surface, despite what might be apparent from the surface. I find this the best way to explain the educational system for a special needs child.

Above the Surface

Jordan is sitting at a desk with her name printed on the top left corner. She is surrounded by people who understand when she speaks. Her backpack hangs in her cubby. She listens to her teacher read a chapter from *Lulu and the Brontosaurus*. When she interrupts to talk about Disney princesses, her teacher skillfully refocuses her.

Below the Surface

After hours of testing, paperwork, and appointments, Zac and I meet with the Committee on Special Education for our school district. We live in a town that allocates funds for special education students and the services required. The committee of administrators, teachers, and therapists assesses Jordan's progress and determines a need for classification. She receives an individualized educational plan (IEP), a legal document describing levels of performance and measurable goals. We meet with the committee annually to determine if the modifications, related services, and specialized instruction are still suitable for her needs. If a situation occurs (i.e., when I was concerned about her navigating the playground equipment at the elementary school), we can call an emergency meeting as needed. Then the committee determines the placement of the child in the classroom to make sure she is learning in the "least restrictive environment." Our school determined that Jordan would benefit from a self-contained classroom, a smaller setting with a higher ratio of teachers to students. This was a struggle for us. We wanted her to be in a larger classroom setting with peer models to aid her progress, but we also knew she would not learn in this environment. We are realistic but hopeful about her educational goals, though we know we have a very social child, and we want her to be happy. In the selected environment, Jordan would receive one-on-one instruction, which she requires to learn, but have fewer interactions with her peers in the building.

This process is exhausting, emotional, and overwhelming. Special needs parents prepare for these appointments, but you never know what is going to happen until you are experiencing them. I have been on both sides of the table as a parent and an educator and I have seen it all: homemade muffins, power suits, translators, educational advocates, tears, lawyers, laughter, and one diaper change (that was us). Mothers are rarely called by their names, but only referred to as their role: *Mom, how did this year go for you?* Educators, specialists, doctors—call us by our names. We were someone before we were this child's parent; and in this room, we need to remember that identity to be able to advocate for our child. Copious notes are taken, and it is a quick game to categorize the importance of a question with the allotted time remaining. It is necessary, taxing, and sweaty.

Suggestions are made for community programs that could be accessed to get further opportunities for socialization and skill building. Schools will provide therapy; however, there are state-funded programs that support further resources, such as respite care, social programs, and educational opportunities.

We were hoping to receive support to give Jordan swim and dance lessons. We were told on first glance that Jordan's scores were probably too high, and she would not receive any of this government support. Too high? Are we talking about the same child? How broken is this system? It's back to finding allies to navigate the system, more paperwork, more testing, and then, like so many parents in our situation—we wait.

As each meeting ends, the paperwork is signed, the documents are filed, and people move on to their next meeting. Yet everything that has been said needs to be processed. There are facts presented that are difficult to swallow and hear about your own child, and yet they must be heard so you can create the next game plan. This is a recursive process: your child changes, their needs change. For Jordan's last IEP, we heard anecdotes of her kindness, her successful transitions, and her new letter recognition. They handed me a piece of paper with the letters of her name. She had worked hard to produce it over several weeks. We had a challenging discussion about her writing deficits and whether it was an achievable goal. Zac and I thanked the committee, gathered our giant binder of paperwork, and walked down the hall toward the exit.

We rarely speak after the meetings—our brains are overloaded by what has been said or, more importantly, what hasn't been acknowledged. Committees need to acknowledge what is below the iceberg. Our pride and our sorrow. Our recognition and our uncertainty. Our effort and our missteps. Our successes and our guilt.

Zac and I passed a bulletin board from a neurotypical classroom, highlighting the letters of gratitude for Thanksgiving that the students had written. I stopped to read the uncertain lettering of a child younger than Jordan, talking about how happy school made him. I clutched Jordan's name sign, remembering that, like all things, gratitude will look a little different in our house.

CHAPTER 31
Dear Teacher

Every few months, I find my handwriting scribbled on the back of an envelope. It lists the names of people I owe a thank-you note. I have every intention of drafting my appreciation; in fact, I look forward to it. However, it is always at the bottom of the to-do list. The only thank-you note I have successfully completed was to Jordan's kindergarten teacher. Sometimes you just have to move your gratitude to the top of the list.

I never imagined that my daughter would have a teacher like you.

The day I learned she was classified as having "special needs," I started scheduling the extensive hours in therapies, learning the new language of IEPs, and acclimating to a "new normal." What I never planned on finding was a stranger who would be totally invested in our child's successes. Someone outside of our circle who would be just as excited when Jordan indicated she needed to use the toilet or successfully transitioned between activities. Someone who took pictures of the first time my daughter drew a straight line or circled the word that started with the first letter of her name because she knew it was remarkable.

I know what the job entails. I might have a different population and age group, but I know the long hours, the changing curriculum, the state mandates, and the emotional demands. I also know of the potential for joy and how badly you need to fight for it. Every day in your classroom, that joy was palpable.

And that is not a small feat.

You created a space where she was not just trying to acclimate to the concept of school, the dynamics of friendship, even her own body, but she was also allowed to be the best version of herself. In your classroom, children are given the space to celebrate what feels natural. You have effortlessly and impeccably created a world that fosters a community and teaches children—some who were told they could never "traditionally" learn. That, dear teacher, is nothing short of magic.

Jordan's educational journey is only just beginning, and you are the vanguard. You have started her on the path to learn that school is not a place of can't and won't, but try and try again. You have instilled the security to know that there may be hard days, but there will always be a welcoming seat in your room. You have, through your daily dedication, skilled expertise, and thoughtful planning, whispered confidence into my own child.

And if that weren't enough, you guided me through the best ways to parent her. Your name became the reason we could get more accomplished at home, because she knew what was expected of her and didn't want to let you down. You not only provided practical solutions, thoughtful recommendations, and empathetic listening, but you also gave me confidence that I could do this as well. Because of you, I could look past the extensive hours of therapy, the new language of IEPs, and my new normal—I could just enjoy time with my child.

There will never be words to acknowledge my gratitude.

As a teacher, I would like to say, "Teach me your secrets." And as a mother, with tears in my eyes, I would like to simply say, "Thank you."

CHAPTER 32
Everyone Needs a Billy

L ong before he was a successful designer in New York City, Billy was my first friend. We would spend our afternoons lost in our imaginations, racing up and down the street between our two houses. We would wait for the bus, retracing the bike path cemented into my sidewalk as if it were a tightrope. After school, we would do our homework, curl up in front of his Christmas tree, and eat his mother's homemade cookies.

It was a very happy childhood. In fact, when I led my students through a creative writing exercise to recall their own memories, my model is always flooded with memories of Billy in the 1980s. The morning we ran from the neighbors shooting BB guns at us, the afternoon I fell into the swimming pool and he tried to save me, and the evening when I had to bike over quickly because his imaginary friend, Toots, had suddenly passed away. Toots deserved a proper burial.

I assumed everyone had a friend like Billy—a spirited, creative companion who was nothing but joy. I would hear his voice outside my house, "Peah [the remnants of a rough nickname], come outside," and I knew an adventure was waiting for us.

Our favorite activity was trick-or-treating. Billy always had the most original costumes, and I would wear the same costume every year: a snake charmer his mom had made for my sister's fourth-grade play. It was so ornate that both my sister and I would wear it until the matching snake, Minerva, began to wear out. Billy and I would run ahead together to collect candy while our parents sauntered behind us, talking. It was a contest to see how many houses we could get to before they sent us home. It was pure joy.

We don't talk much these days, as most childhood friendships tend to wane, but he was the first person I thought of on the morning of Jordan's first day of kindergarten. My crystallized memory of sitting next to Billy on the bus juxtaposed to her isolated face in the window. My eagerness to ask my mom to call his house for an afternoon playdate compared to solitary sorting of erasers every afternoon. Would Jordan ever have a Billy?

The sadness blindsided me. We had come so far, recognizing her potential to learn and enrolling her in countless hours of therapy to help her meet her potential—but we never stopped to consider friendship.

I read a story once of a mom of a special needs child who took her daughter to a school sporting event and noticed all the girl's classmates were laughing together, recounting their days. When she looked down, she saw her own child in a wheelchair, happily playing alone with her toy ponies. She discusses her realization that friendship was a social construction that she was accustomed to as a mother, not the one her daughter necessarily subscribed to. Her daughter didn't feel isolated, because she was content in the activity she had chosen for herself.

Was I projecting my own memories of childhood onto Jordan? Did she desire a friend as I had, or was it just what I expected for her?

My confidence decreased during our first school event. Jordan was in a self-contained class, which meant that, during the day, she met only a few people, most of whom also had special needs. She did not have a lot of interaction with general education students, which meant she didn't know a lot of people in town. Since no one from her class attended the event, she was left alone in a sea of swimming children. Rather than participating, she quietly hung back. "We can go home now."

Does she realize all the other children have someone to sit with? Is this what happens during school? Is she lonely?

I cried in the car. It was my first big cry in years. Due to my new tough demeanor, not much swayed me these days, but the realization that my child might be lonely was too much to take. We had created an incredible support system of people for her, but they were our people, not hers.

I cried for the childhood I wanted her to have. I cried for the disappointment she might not have felt. I cried for my inability to know how to help her.

I could rationalize why it was okay to remain insular. After all, she saw a lot of people during her school days and at her after-school events. It took all the energy she had just to get to 4:00 p.m., so having a playdate on top of that would just be more arduous than amusing. It was acceptable to remain in her cocoon.

I was also hiding in my cocoon. I was ready to reenter the world, but I didn't know how to begin. I felt as if I had been living in a fallout shelter for the past decade and didn't know the language. I was a little too eager, a little too depleted, a little too desperate.

We were invited to a neighborhood party and I was so excited to see her play with kids her age, I cried while thanking the hostess for the invitation. No one is too eager to invite the lady who cried over the cheese puffs bowl. When I met another parent who had a child with special needs, I was so excited to commiserate that I went home second-guessing whether I had talked too much. I knew there were other parents just like me who were seeking relationships for their children. Someone should make a Tinder for us: Tired Mom Seeks Friend. I knew I just needed to keep putting myself out there. I mean, I have a high tolerance for challenging tasks; making new friends in my thirties shouldn't be one of them.

Jordan did, in fact, not make just one new friend; she made several. She found kind boys and girls in her class to spend her recess with. According to the necklace we had made at a craft fair, one special girl was her new BFF, Manami. Jordan's and Manami's lives became intertwined in the most beautiful of ways. Manami's family was temporarily living in the United States for a few years before her father's work would move them back to Japan. She was in Jordan's self-contained class, and Jordan was obsessed with her.

Their dance teacher described their relationship perfectly: a constant couple's skate. They were often holding hands, not speaking to each other, gliding through life together. They were opposites in most ways: Jordan's tousled hair flying out from underneath her favorite winter hat, next to Manami's beautifully braided ponytail. Jordan's boisterous cheering and nonstop chatter complemented Manami's reserved demeanor. Manami helped rebuild the LEGO block pieces Jordan struggled to hold while Jordan guided her bestie into the center of every dance party, even if there was no music. Their friendship was nothing short of magical.

This year, Manami and Jordan went trick-or-treating together. Without exchanging a word, they complimented each other's costumes and giggled their way from house to house. By the time we hit the fourth house, a group of neighborhood kids ran by. There must have been about twenty-five children, in a sea of colors and props, racing to see who could get the candy first. Most of these children didn't even notice our girls, but one little boy stopped and said, "Hi, Manami. Hi, Jordan. See you at school."

Undeterred, Jordan took Manami's hand and pulled her toward the next house. They remained hand in hand, walking through the neighborhood together. They ran ahead while we parents strolled behind them, talking. We made it to about ten houses before they were both fatigued. It was pure joy.

Manami will not be trick-or-treating with us again. Her family moved back to Japan, and she and Jordan are across the world from each other. Jordan knows she is not in school, but I do not know if she has the language to understand the permanence of it. "Manami is coming next week from Japan," she tells me.

I am hopeful we have enough pictures to relive the memories until the ache stops. I am hopeful modern technology will connect them. And I am hopeful that the small boy who stopped to say hello this year might be free for trick-or-treating next October.

CHAPTER 33
The Effusive Gene

My parents captured my childhood in one simple phrase in my baby book: *It appears that at eighteen months, Leah will be a chatterbox.* My natural disposition was that of cheerfulness. Home videos from my 1985 nursery school graduation showcase four-year-old me with a mullet of curls, joyfully participating in the group song, bopping in my seat, completely unaware I was the only one in the class not wailing. I was just always peppy. It was innate to who I was. This was clearly a genetic trait. Jordan revealed her interpretation of being a peppy chatterbox. The frequency of her speech was increasing, as a result of her increasing breath support. It gave her more opportunities to talk about the same topic multiple times a day. Specialists call it "perseverating," or continually repeating an idea or behavior.

This first conversation was only about the pop singer Ariana Grande.

"Jordan, would you like chicken soup or pizza for dinner?"

"R-Grande."

Some might say she was obsessed. She wanted her ponytail to match Ariana's and desperately needed to learn her dance moves—despite how provocative they were. Our closest family and friends would send her magazine clippings, YouTube videos, and even a full book about

Ariana Grande's life. The boys even said "R-Grande" as one of their earlier words. Totally typical: *Mama, Dada, dog,* famous pop singer with a trademark ponytail.

When Disney's *Descendants* came on the scene, Jordan soon forgot the days of "fabric free" dance videos, as I once saw on a sign in Texas, and moved on to Mal and Evie, the children of famous villains. She learned the entire plot, backstory, and character history of the show. This made for some awkward grocery store interactions. One time she shouted, "Evil Queen has locked me in the car!" and I hoped the cashier realized it was merely role-play. This was one time I was glad the cashier could not understand her.

She often shocked us by stopping a roomful of people to exclaim, "Excuse me, I have big news. Drumroll please."

Shy was not in her vocabulary. She would not continue until everyone was drumming on the surface of their choice. She would shout until she got the attention she demanded. It was like she'd learned the teacher trick: *I'll wait.*

"Okay?" Her voice would crescendo with excitement. "Who is Mal's dad?"

I was not sure she even cared who the father was, but we'd had this discussion eight hundred times. That is not hyperbole. It was discussed three, eight, fourteen times a day. My uncle even took time off from his medical practice to watch Disney's *Descendants* so he could talk to her about it.

We continue to encourage her functional discussions, and while we love the conversations, even her most beloved community needed a break from pontificating the familial heritage of a fictional heroine.

This was how we landed on the next fixation: American presidents.

Jordan learned about the presidents in first grade. President's Day came and went the first time through, but by the second time, she was celebrating her favorite presidents: Washington, Jackson, and her favorite new president, Tom Chester. (He apparently didn't get a lot of attention in the history books.)

If we were holding up the line at the grocery store, it was because Jordan needed to know when the cashier was born so she could match the president. At the doctor with the flu? Perfect time to tell the nurse born in 1981 that she was a Reagan baby. An infant spotted at the park—Jordan would run up and shout "Donald Trump baby," usually leaving a perplexed look on the parent's face. Her question even prompted a debate about politics at the neurologist's office.

Sometimes people needed me to translate for her; other times they understood her perfectly. It depended on the situation and how much energy Jordan had to articulate her words.

Jordan's teacher recently shared, "Jordan's energy makes everyone feel welcomed. She has such an amazing impact on everyone she meets."

Jordan is innately drawn to people. But she needs to refuel before the next performance. Therefore, we spend many long days at home just talking about the topic of the day.

"Mommy." She giggled upside down on the chair. "Mommy. It's important."

"What, honey?"

"Mommy, who is Mal's dad?"

"Jordan! I figured it out. It's Obama!"

When Jordan laughs so hard, she collapses onto the floor, revealing a tiny dimple by her left eye. It is contagious.

Sometimes this parenting thing is a breeze.

CHAPTER 34
When Life Bites
You in the Butt

While I frantically cut the last of the grapes into the smallest possible bites, I shooed away a familiar feeling. My daughter had once again bitten me on the butt.

She was hungry. In the middle of explaining to Oliver why I couldn't change his shirt while wearing oven mitts, and calming a hysterical Austin because he couldn't go outside to eat all the raindrops, Jordan demonstrated the signs of being over-hungry. I had missed my window.

I was not sure at this point if it was more unnerving that I was bitten or that it didn't faze me. It had become the norm. Her mouth was the exact height of my derriere, she had learned it didn't hurt me, and it immediately made her needs known. She was about to lose it. Her usually sweet disposition would soon be replaced by a shrieking stranger. I de-escalated the situation by handing her a perfectly cut bowl of grapes and she echoed the calm in my voice with the gratitude in hers.

As I turned back to the kitchen counter, I felt another bite.

I pulled back, this time to see Austin, very much over his desire for raindrops, standing there, smiling, holding out his hands, waiting for his portion.

I used my formal parenting training. "We don't bite."

"Okay. Grapes, please."

Next week. Same butt. Different son.

"We don't bite."

"Okay. Grapes, please."

This was a ripple effect of raising a special needs child. All this time, I was concerned about managing Jordan's behaviors, but I never realized her twin brothers were watching, studying, learning. They did not see her limitations, only her actions. They didn't know how incredible it was that she'd learned to stand independently at the counter or that her yelling at me was something I'd only dreamed of hearing one day. In some cases, I condoned behaviors that would otherwise be unsuitable, and my sons would learn those behaviors too. If she received a bowl of grapes by biting, they would too. They weren't acting out. They thought this was the way things were run around here—no "please," no "thank you," just bite.

We wanted our impressionable boys to understand as best they could. While we knew it would be a long time before they understood the complexity of Jordan's diagnosis, we tried to explain at an early age why Jordan had to wear the same hat every day, why she needed another wig, or why she still wore diapers at night. When it was time for Jordan's nightly medicine, Jordan asked for her "doctor brothers," who enthusiastically administered her premeasured dosage and milk. These toddler boys were not ready to learn all the details of their sister's needs, but they knew when she was struggling because her favorite pair of pajamas were still in the dryer or we were out of Oreo cookies. They knew she needed a distraction.

One challenging afternoon when rain made it impossible to play outside, Austin and Oliver ran to the dress bin while Zac tried to calm Jordan. The boys called me to join them for a surprise. They stuck their tiny faces in my ear, raised their eyebrows, and whispered in such tiny voices, I had no idea what they were saying. Their intentions were clear, though—it was time to make Jordan giggle.

The boys made us sit in circle time, just like they did in class. They passed out a wig to each member of the family. It helped that we had so many to choose from. "Jordie, you get pink. It's your favorite. Daddy, turn on Jordie's music."

Most people don't end the day with teeth marks on their rear, but most people also don't end the day with a dance party and coordinating wigs. As Jordan twirled around in Zac's arms, thanking her brothers for the party, it was then that I was glad the boys were watching.

CHAPTER 35
Circle Time on Route 80

It was ironic that I got pulled over for speeding, because I usually drive no faster than fourteen miles per hour, in a minivan, sometimes in the left lane. I'm that person.

This was one of my first longer trips without Zac in the car. Most of my stories of havoc happen when he is at a work event and I'm trying to do this parenting thing by myself. I was lucky that when Zac was home, he was such a hands-on husband, or else we would have needed our own wing in the emergency room. In this instance, Zac was at a conference and I wasn't quite ready for an entire weekend by myself. I was getting better at asking for help, though.

We headed to New Jersey to visit Grandma and Grandpa, while I threw food toward hungry mouths, checked my directions, and changed songs on the radio. I was doing far too much, too quickly. Not a good idea.

When the police officer approached my car, the look of surprise was very visible on his face. I was in my pajamas with some peanut butter on my sleeve. In the rear of the van was Jordan belting "A Whole New World" in her Jasmine wig that made her look like a cast member of *Children of the Corn*. Her singing was causing the sobbing siblings in the middle of the van to try to escape her serenades: "No, Jordie. Stop!"

"Good morning, Officer," I croaked.

[Inaudible. It is impossible to hear someone speak when there are three screaming children in the back seat.]

"I'm so sorry. I can't hear you." I frantically moved the oversized tote bag of food on the front seat to access the glove compartment for my registration.

"Could you excuse me, Officer?" I turned around and yelled above the noise: "Can I have everyone's attention? We have pulled over to the side of the highway because I wanted to introduce you to someone."

[Immediate silence.]

"Who, Mommy?" Jordan's chin innocently asked. Her eyes were completely covered by her terrifying wig.

"Well, this is a police officer and he is here to make sure people are following the law. Raise your hand if you have learned about police officers at school."

Three hands immediately rose in the air. The teacher in me was so proud.

They couldn't contain their excitement and rained questions on him.

"Do you know firemen?"

"Do you know Batman?"

"Do you know Jafar?"

I smiled in his direction as if saying, *Please do not be upset with this. I am not sure how to explain why we are pulled over. We have a routine set for every day, and this isn't one of them. I don't want to scare them. Also, there is a decapitated deer head on the road directly in front of us and I'm not sure what to do about it. Please pretend this is a classroom visit and not the side of the road on Route 80.*

He smiled back; thank goodness. "Hello, everyone. I am your community helper. I just wanted to introduce myself to you all. I'm going to take these pieces of paper to my car and I'll be right back."

As the officer approached his vehicle, Oliver said, "This was fun. Thank you for taking us here."

"Of course, honey. I thought you would like it."

The officer approached our car. He returned my license and registration—no ticket. With a smile, he said, "Thank you for visiting. I hope you enjoyed learning about police officers today." Then he turned to me and said, "Slow down, please."

I'm trying, Mr. Community Helper. I'm trying.

CHAPTER 36
Every Parent Everywhere

Tonight, my son was a helicopter. He was Batman. He was a dancing monkey. He was everything but tired.

I, on the other hand, was an exhausted mother.

A day that began with the 5:00 a.m. treadmill, thirty-five graded poetry projects, three meetings, one swim class, and two cracked eggs on the floor (*No, honey, that isn't paint*) needed to end with a little bit of quiet time. Not being used as a landing pad.

I was ornery, and with each passing moment I was not the mother I wanted to be. I was tired of being the only one listening to the bedtime story. I was frustrated by the tiny fingers stabbing my eyeballs. I was defeated by the third time they had thrown my glasses against the wall. I was surrendering.

They are only young once. You will never get this time back. They won't be little forever.

Too bad. I desperately wanted to escape this diaper-pail dungeon.

But all they wanted to do was make the toddler version of *If You Give a Mouse a Cookie*. If you hit your toe against the wall, you will need a bandage to put on it. And if you get a bandage, then you will have to turn on the light to see what color it is. And if you turn the light on to see what color it is, your other son will see and then need one too because he feels left out. But he is afraid of bandages, so you will have to get him a sticker so he doesn't cry. And now that the light is on, they will realize their bellies are hungry. And if you bring them a banana, they will need some water to go with it. And if you bring them water, they will spill it on their pants and need new ones. But not any pants, only the pair of Batman pants they are already wearing. And if you cannot produce a magical second pair of these Batman pants, they will continue to cry so loudly, they will wake up their sister. Because it is now 9:00 p.m. and you have been at this for the past two hours.

And on a night like this, when all requests were finally handled, as I pulled the door shut, Oliver whispered, "Mommy."

"Yes, honey."

Austin snored next to him, finally asleep like he fell asleep in the middle of a dance battle.

"Mommy," Oliver whispered gently, "I can't go to bed without singing my Shabbat song."

I pulled the door shut, and my frustration released to a giggle. Apparently, he was really connecting to his preschool program at the temple. I deserved my alone time, but I could try to remember to enjoy the chaos while it was happening. We've had so many struggles, inevitably there will be more, and ultimately I am grateful for their healthy, rambunctious bodies. But sometimes I'd rather appreciate them tomorrow after a good night's rest.

Now, if you will excuse me, it looks like Oliver has awoken his brother with his passionate rendition of "Shabbat Shalom, Hey!"

CHAPTER 37
Parenting Magic

I was reading through the *New York Times* and saw a series on "parenting successes." I read through relatable comments about bedtime, feeding picky eaters, and surviving long car rides. It's the universal truth of parenthood: looking for opportunities to celebrate and commiserate.

When I thought about our strongest parenting wins, they all occurred when Jordan had had "too much." Overtired, over-hungry, or overstimulated. The concept of waiting is at times literally impossible. It makes her belligerent, and my effervescent, giggling girl disappears. Imagine the way you feel awaiting your number at the DMV. It is like that every day in her body. We don't cater to her every whim, but there is a difference between "I don't feel like waiting" and "I can't wait at this very moment."

I'm a bit superstitious to state these parental wins aloud. The magic of the *kenahora* follows us in this house, the Yiddish concept of "bad luck." You say aloud, "Phew, the baby is finally sleeping through the night" only to suddenly hear wailing. "No one has been sick in such a long time" as projectile vomit hits your face. You get the idea. It's like the Jewish version of Alanis Morissette's song, "Ironic."

But perhaps these parenting wins could help someone else when their child is also "too much," so it's worth the risk.

It was Zac who received the first win.

Jordan was having a tantrum as a result of sensory overload. When this happens, there are a handful of toys that will calm her. We keep them stowed away in a box for emergencies; however, if she discovers the box, all the items lose their ability to redirect her, as she has already seen them. We had finally located a spot for the box where she could not find it. During this instance, she would not leave Zac's side as he was trying to get her something from the box to help recalibrate her.

"Honey, I have to get you something," Zac reassured her.

"I want it!"

"Yes. It is in the closet, but [thank goodness for his improv classes in college] the closet only appears when Daddy is alone."

(He has never been so sexy.)

"Okay, Daddy." She walked into her room and patiently waited for the item.

Then there was the time the little lady refused to eat anything. It was a combination of losing a tooth, having another come in, and fully avoiding food. When she turned down her favorite foods—chicken soup, strawberry ices, and what she calls "Fourth of July" (a combination of berries and Goldfish crackers)—we were screwed. However, she showed interest in gelatin. Great solution: it's a meal and an activity. We measured, poured, and stirred, and then I discovered it would be ready in ninety minutes, not the instant one we had bargained for.

"I want it," Jordan begged.

"I know. Let's take a bath first," I suggested. Validate and redirect.

"No. One, two, three. It's ready. I want it!!!"

A little eye contact and a plan was made (I had taken those improv classes too). I would distract her for ten minutes and Zac would race to the grocery store to grab premade Jell-O.

"Jordan, calm down. It's okay. The reason it is going to take so long is because we forgot our magic potion. We are so silly."

While Zac snuck out the back door, I sat with the three kids and our imaginary cauldron. The store is three minutes away. I imagined him sprinting down the aisles, mumbling, "No time. Need Jell-O." He hadn't moved that fast when I was in labor.

We held our imaginary wands—well, three imaginary wands and Austin's muffin—to shout our favorite magical words.

"Abracadabra!"

"Bibbidi-bobbidi-boo!"

"Expelliarmus!"

We did the "Magic Jell-O Dance" (use your imagination) and *POOF*! Ten minutes later, the Jell-O was ready and in her bowl.

"I did it!" she shouted, her face full of red goo.

Yes, you did Jordan. And so did we.

Sometimes the plan backfires. On one Mother's Day she was too excited, the anticipation of visitors was too much for her, and she couldn't contain herself. When this happens, we have learned that Jordan is the most responsive to input on her head. We learned it was why she put the dance skirt around her forehead rather than her waist and why she would beg us to tie ribbons into her hair so she could feel the fabric flowing down her face. That's how she figured out how to make the head of a doll a ponytail holder so the hair of the doll would feel like her own. It became the easiest solution for everyone when we discovered wigs. She now has one in every color and length and will spend hours admiring her locks in the mirror.

However, when even a wig won't do the trick, I learned to momentarily calm her with Snapchat, finding filters of her with straight hair. Her excitement inspired my terrible brainstorm—straightening her hair. It would be time-consuming and make her feel special, as it is something I never let her do. Not just because we embrace our curls in this house, but the heat wasn't great for her little head. She sat in front of the mirror and told her imaginary YouTube fans that her mom was going to use the straightener. With each piece I straightened, she shouted, "Oh yeah, baby!" at her reflection and blew kisses to herself.

"Do you like it, Jordan?" I asked when the styling was complete.

"I don't like it. I love it." She changed into her favorite dress, jean jacket, and sparkly boots, and demanded the family watch her in a runway show while she twirled through the kitchen shouting, "This is my true look!"

The problem with raising a fashionista who sees the world as her runway means you can no longer settle for an everyday look. Her normal head of gorgeous spiral curls was now "too boring," and living without her straight hair was enough to warrant a full temper tantrum every day. I learned early on with behavior modification that if I let her win the battles, I would lose the war. So I held firm. Well, almost. I made a small addendum.

"Jordan, you can straighten the front two pieces of your hair every Saturday. For your birthday, you can straighten the entire thing."

She cheered as she took me into the "salon," our 1950s bathroom. She blew kisses at herself in the mirror while I took out the iron.

"There you go. You look adorable."

"I don't look adorable, Mommy. I look fashionable."

She turned, as if on the end of a catwalk in imaginary high heels, and sashayed down the hall, with a purposeful hair flip.

Parenting wins need to be celebrated whenever they happen. Even if that means my child feels beautiful rocking a Kate Gosselin hairstyle. Straight in the front, curly party in the back.

CHAPTER 38
The Secret to Parenting—Lying

My dear friend told her son if he used her fancy shampoo, he would grow boobs. He stopped using it immediately. About two weeks later he said innocently, "Mom, I think Dad has been using your shampoo."

I always loved this story because it was such a great lie with hilarious results. Who knows how long it will linger? The father in this story has a great sense of humor. No harm done.

I, too, was raised with some harmless lies. I will never live down my ninth-grade enthusiastic response to the definition of *karma* with my aunt Judy's system for finding a perfect parking spot: "parking karma." Nor my debacle of having two right chopsticks and needing to ask the waiter to trade one out for a left one. These stories were not debunked until I was—embarrassingly—in college. But again, no harm. Meanwhile, I was thrilled to have a chance to learn the art of the parental lie. After the years I had been having, if the biggest concern of my day was how to fabricate the truth—it was a welcomed relief.

Oliver's beloved monkey, Bobo, was a casualty of a chaotic trip to the store. We were having a day enjoying an outing to Five Below. The price was right for our budget. We left, only destroying one display of soccer balls, with a toy for each child, but no stuffed monkey.

The frantic search for Bobo began at bedtime. Not in the car. Not in the backyard. Not in the fridge or the freezer. Not under the bed. I called the store in a panic.

"Thank you for calling Five Below. How may I help you?"

"Have you seen Bobo?!" I screeched.

"Excuse me?"

"Oh, um. Bobo. It's my son's monkey. He is three years old. My son, not the monkey. It's just a head without arms or legs."

"Excuse me?"

"My son's stuffed animal. We think he left it in the middle of the ball display. It's sort of a bedtime emergency."

"We have a pink elephant with no arms."

"No, thank you."

By the time I had walked the fifteen steps back to my son's room, I had already ordered a backup Bobo on Amazon. Thank you, Prime membership.

I shook my head at my husband and brightly chirped, "Guess what, Oliver? Bobo went on vacation!"

Austin shouted, "Just like when we go to Texas!" He seemed very jealous of Bobo.

I proceeded to explain that Bobo had so much fun in the store that he stayed to ride on motorcycles and would be back in two business days—I mean Tuesday.

"But I think Bobo is sad without me," Oliver whimpered.

"Well, just like you were sad when Mommy and Daddy went away for a few days and you missed us, you knew we would be back," Zac encouraged him.

"No, Daddy. I didn't miss you guys. I only miss Bobo."

Well, at least we knew where we stood.

This was our observant child. This was the boy who noticed if he got the wrong-size fork at dinner or if the crayons had been changed in the box. He would surely notice a replacement Bobo.

The next morning, he woke up to a postcard from Bobo. It was a sheet of computer paper with a screenshot of Bobo pasted on top of a cartoon motorcycle. It looked like I had spent exactly one minute making it, which was accurate.

> *Dear Oliver,*
> *I have missed you so much while I've been on vacation. I found this great blue motorcycle that I chose because I know it is your favorite color. I cannot wait to see you later. I might look a little different after my travels—but I am still your same Bobo! I love you.*
> *Love,*
> *Bobo*

He carried the postcard around with him all day. "Look at Bobo riding on the motorcycle. He is having so much fun."

Tuesday evening, Bobo returned. "Look, Mama, Bobo came back." He hugged him deeply. "I missed you."

I closed the door to hear him chatting. "How was your vacation, Bobo? Did you wear a helmet? I missed you so much."

Note, my dear Oliver, when you are old enough to read this book, you will have learned the truth of your beloved Bobo. Also, it is possible to open a cookie tin without eating three pieces of broccoli first. Love, your crafty mama.

CHAPTER 39
Police and Crutches and Wigs, Oh My

Today's challenge: Party City. One Elsa wig.

There was a concern that Jordan's blank stares during her eye therapy sessions could be absence seizures. We thought she might just be bored. She wasn't really engaged jumping from footprint to footprint during her sessions. The pediatric ophthalmologist, however, was insistent: "I think she is having absence seizures."

We made an appointment with the neurologist who ordered an overnight EEG to get a better sense of what was happening inside her head. When she walked us through the upcoming procedure, explaining the wires, the gauze, and the main rule that Jordan could not pull them off, we knew this was going to be impossible.

"Sometimes, children like to wear hats so they can't see the EEG cap," the neurologist suggested.

"That might work. She loves an accessory."

When my mom told me about a hat she had seen with an Elsa wig attached to it, I knew we couldn't do our overnight stay at the hospital without it.

While Zac was at his afterschool rehearsal, I decided it was the perfect time for our afternoon adventure: 10 percent, we needed the wig; 10 percent, I was a glutton for punishment; and 80 percent, I craved the control. There was so much in life that I could not control, that I was demanding to keep what I could in my clutches. I could not be sure how Jordan would respond to the EEG, but I could be sure she had an Elsa wig on when it happened. In hindsight, it wasn't my best idea as I had also recently broken my ankle and needed to take the kids while I was on crutches and in a boot. I was a mom on a mission. And stubborn (very stubborn).

They walked into the store calmly. Upon the opening of the automatic doors, the kids must have thought they heard the starter's pistol discharge for the one-hundred-yard dash at the Olympics, and they toddled in three different directions. I found Jordan first, underneath a purple wig, while Oliver was climbing a shelf to reach a toy car and Austin was trying to unwrap seven lollipops. "Yum, Mommy."

I lured each one into the shopping cart with M&M's from the bottom of the diaper bag. Five minutes later, Elsa wig in hand, we hobbled to the car.

"This was quite the adventure," I declared as I buckled Jordan into her car seat. "I'm exhausted."

After a moment, I added, "Austin, come sit in your seat," and I bribed him with yet another M&M, this time from my pocket.

I threw my backpack and crutches into the front seat and attempted to grab Oliver. He was too busy trying to drive the car and pushing all the buttons in the driver's seat. When he was finally in my grasp, I managed to squeeze him into the car seat and secure the final buckle. I closed the door.

I leaned against the car, exhaled, and said aloud, "Okay, we did it." Favorite moment of the day—children calm behind those secured car seat harnesses.

I walked to the driver's door. It was locked. I returned to the passenger side. Locked. Passenger doors, trunk. Locked. Locked.

Oliver noticed immediately. His voice wavered, "Mommy, open."

There are days when you think, *I really have a hold on my life*. Then there are others when you lock your children in the car. I couldn't lose it; the kids were watching. I decided to make it an adventure.

"Mommy is so silly, and she left the keys in the car. Can anyone unbuckle their seat belts and reach Mommy's keys?"

Luckily, my phone was in my coat pocket. I dialed 911. No answer. I wish I'd made up that detail for the sake of building suspense.

I quickly assessed the situation. It was thirty-five degrees outside. They were not trapped in a hot car. We were in a parking lot. The emergency phone service apparently didn't think this was an emergency. My children each had at least seven M&M's in their bellies to keep them full for twenty minutes.

I called Zac. "So, I locked the kids in the car. We're okay, but I need you."

"Wait, what?"

"We are in the Party City parking lot. Can you bring the spare key? Sorry!"

I hung up and then shouted through the car window, "Okay, Daddy is on his way with the keys!"

I tried 911 again. They would send a car. For the next twenty minutes, I waited to see who would arrive first. I alternated pep talks for each of my children.

For Jordan: "Mommy will put your hat on as soon as she can."

For Austin: "It's okay, honey, stop crying."

For Oliver: "No, Mommy isn't mad that you can't open your buckle. I know you are trying."

I attracted a crowd.

Strangers all over the parking lot were coming to my aid. One mother rubbed my back and offered me a hanger to try to put through the window; it was velvet. "I'll just stay with you if that's okay," she offered.

"We'll be okay," I explained.

I was worried her kindness was going to unmoor me. I only break in front of the people who know how to pick up my pieces. It is a short but sturdy list. I wasn't sure if this stranger wanted to be added to the list, but I would have done the same for her, so I leaned into her kindness.

A man and his child approached our car with a toolbox. By the time the police arrived, I had four people trying to pry my window open and a car of screaming, terrified children.

Unfortunately, the police did not have the tools they needed to get car doors open because so many people had been litigious about the damage it had caused to their vehicles. They could call emergency support, but it was at the scene of an accident, so we waited another twenty minutes for Zac.

Inhale. We are fine. I relied on my coping mechanisms for de-escalating a situation.

Use facts and data. My daughter cannot open her seat belt because she has a rare genetic syndrome and struggles with her fine motor skills.

Find empathy. When one of the helpers told me she had a child with special needs, but "he grew out of it," I decided it wasn't time for my lecture about studies behind disabilities. Some people have more maladaptive strategies than I do to handle the truth.

Collect yourself. I graciously thanked the men and encouraged them to keep destroying my passenger window, with the hope that they would be victorious first. I calmed Jordan's cries, reassured Oliver that it was not his fault his three-year-old muscles weren't strong enough to push on the red button, and reminded Austin that Mommy was calling in superhero Daddy to save us.

When Zac's car pulled up, he tossed me the key and I won a world record for getting three children out of their car seats—while wearing a boot. I smothered their sweaty faces with my hugs.

"Mommy is so proud of you!"

Tears ran down my cheeks as I began to release my fear. My helpers lovingly said goodbye and the crowd dissipated.

"Daddy!" Austin cheered and grabbed the key fob to see what button he pushed to save the day.

"Mommy?" Jordan prompted as we stood outside of the car, huddled together.

"Yes, sweetie?" I was ready for her to say something profound. It's usually in these moments that she says something so endearing. I needed her wisdom this time.

"Mommy. We were inside the car."

"Yes, sweetie."

"Okay. Before we go, can I also get a *blue* wig?"

CHAPTER 40
Only the Rarest for Our Girl ... and Make It French

"It could be like a vacation," I said to Zac as we packed our bags for the hospital. He rolled his eyes at me. I don't think twenty-four hours in a hospital room keeping our child from removing EEG electrodes from her hair was his idea of a vacation.

"Well, I bet we can at least get takeout," he said after a moment.

It would be our first time with just Jordan since the boys had been born. The circumstances weren't ideal, but once she got settled, there would be nothing to do but play—just the three of us. Something we hadn't done in years.

We knew this wasn't easy for any child, let alone one with high sensory needs. Brushing her teeth was one of the most painful activities of the day. Brushing her hair was out of the question. We didn't know if she was even capable of sitting still while dozens of wires were affixed to her head. We didn't have a choice. This was the only way to find out if she was having seizures, and that could be a matter of life and death. We hoped our Elsa hat really contained some magic; we were going to need it.

Once we were settled into our room, the technician came to explain the procedure. We had used our social story to show Jordan the steps to get her new "hat," as we called it. A wire would dip into the paste and then kiss her head. Wire one. *Dip dip.* She pulled it off immediately. Wire one (take two). *Dip dip.* She threw it across the room. This was never going to happen. Maybe there was something they could give her to calm her.

The technician could read my mind. "We can do this, Jordan," he said with patience in his voice.

It took one person to hold her body down, one person to hold her hands down, and two people to attach the twenty-five electrodes to her head. With each wire, she was able to nibble on her cookie, watch some of her tablet, and talk more about the hat we were building for her. Somehow, we made it through the process of building the hat.

"It is time to let the hat start kissing your head," the technician explained. "One more step until we see your new hat."

I could really kiss the medical professionals who play along with our games. It makes everyone's lives so much easier.

He carefully wrapped gauze around Jordan's head, gathered the wires together, and allowed them to run down her back like the long locks she wished she had. Because they were also encased in gauze, she could not see what they really were—the wires just looked like long, white hair. Then he put Jordan's blue Elsa hat—with the accompanying long, white locks—on her head. When Jordan looked in the mirror, there was no evidence of the probes, paste, or procedure. She looked like a snow princess.

"Let's go play," she said as she pulled us into the game room.

For the next twenty-four hours, we focused only on Jordan and making sure she didn't remove her Elsa wig. We had a visit from a music therapist, made some Popsicle stick sculptures, and watched a mermaid movie. We ate takeout, sat at the foot of her bed, and told stories. If we didn't remember why we were there—it was almost a vacation.

It was hard for her to sleep in a new space, even with her fabulous hat. After everyone's sleepless night, the neurologist confirmed the EEG results that Jordan had epilepsy. And because this little one must be fabulous, she had to make sure she had a rare type of epilepsy with a French name. (If you are going to have more than one diagnosis, it's best to have them coordinate.)

We did not see the charm then. We were only absorbing facts. They were called absence seizures, or petit mal seizures, which translates to "little evil." Accurate name. The results showed her brain was spiking 90 percent of the time she slept, meaning her body was rarely at rest. It also meant there wasn't an opportunity for her brain to absorb the information she was acquiring all day, as a brain without epilepsy would. This detail broke my heart. As a result of the hypotonia, or low tone, caused by the cri du chat, Jordan's body was already fatigued. The thought that it was never really getting to rejuvenate made me feel her weariness. On top of it, how hard must she have been working to make the gains she was making, especially if her brain was working overtime to store and retrieve information?

This diagnosis birthed my new motto: scared but prepared. Most of our worries had been about Jordan's development, not her health directly. Despite some terrifying choking incidents she'd had as a baby, which were rectified by her incredible feeding therapists, we knew Jordan was physically safe. The diagnosis of epilepsy added a new stress we hadn't prepared for. When she went to bed, I couldn't sleep, just in case I needed to check the monitor. When she left for school, I felt nervous that they didn't have the correct protocol if she had a seizure. It was a new layer of fatigue for the constant worry.

Keeping it controlled would happen eventually, once they figured out the correct dosage of medication.

"Great, let's get her started," Zac and I said to the doctor.

"Okay. We will give her a dose and then see you in four months to see how it is working."

"And how do you check if it is working?"

She paused. "She will need another EEG. Probably every six months."

That day, after hearing the news, my prepared mom went to Party City and bought out all their Elsa wig hats. It looked as if we would be needing them.

CHAPTER 41
Night, Lon

In my ninth-grade English class, my students study the concept of morality. I created an effective (but terrible) acronym to help them understand how an individual's morality is shaped—PMS: people, moments, and setting. These are the three factors that shape the moral choices we make in our society and our ability to become an upstander.

I was thinking a lot about this for my own life, especially after Jordan's diagnosis. It felt like our family had been given a few too many of these defining moments. We didn't want our resilience tested any further. Yet it was balanced by the other two letters. We had strong medical systems, supportive family and friends, and models in our life that showed us how to respond to adversity.

After we received Jordan's newest diagnosis, I called one of my *P*s, my cousin Lonnie. While we were leaving the hospital in New York, he was being admitted to one in New Jersey.

He was a decade older than I was and taught me things I didn't know I needed to learn. He was the one to *inform* me that if I didn't move my arms when I walked, I wouldn't go anywhere, so I had to propel them forward to gain momentum. Imagine Frankenstein's monster carrying heavy jugs of water with full-arm casts. (I almost took out someone's eye at my preschool graduation.) Then he showed me how to deflect unwanted advances from boys, what Alanis Morissette was singing about in that theater, and the proper way to pour a beer. He knew I was more sentimental than my sister, and that he could get away with tricking me, but then he would always check in with how I was really doing; it is what any brother figure would do. He had always had this balance. He said it is what happens when you battle Hodgkin's lymphoma at a young age and live to tell about it. I don't remember his first battle with cancer, just Transformers and cootie games. When it returned this time, in a new form, it was more than his body could take.

The last time I saw him, I was at a loss for words for the first time in our relationship. I didn't recognize him without his casual banter. I had seen him in pain, fatigued, and cranky after a nap, but I had never seen him dying. I didn't know what questions I wanted to ask him or what memories he wanted to make sure I held on to. Instead, I sat on the corner of his bed with staccato phrases, telling him about the boys and about Jordan's recent battle. He mustered enough strength to tell me she would be okay. She had proven herself to be a fighter. *I guess it runs in the family.*

There are selfish reasons I miss him.

He knew me before I knew myself. When my children were having temper tantrums, he would casually laugh and remind me I used to do the same thing. Then he would do something to make the kids laugh and the tantrum would end. It's always been his way. There is a photo of me and Rachel in our hot-pink, wool sailor dresses at his bar mitzvah, positioned directly in the middle of gawky thirteen-year-old boys in muted brown suits. Rachel, age five, is vibrantly smiling; I, however, appear a bit more overwhelmed at the scene. Lonnie's arms are wrapped around me, as if the photo almost whispers, *Leah, I got you.* Except, my beloved cousin wouldn't have shown his endearment with quite as much sentiment. It would have sounded something more like, *Hey, noodge, smile for this picture or I'll tickle your armpits.* I inherited this beloved Yiddish nickname for "pest" because I was dreadful after I woke up from a nap, a quality I ironically learned from him.

He knew the value of family. After college, Lonnie moved into our basement and commuted to his job in Manhattan. He kept his high school cousins entertained with stories about Rollerblading over the George Washington Bridge and letting us paint his toenails to match his Baja hoodie. He teased Rachel after our grandfather's lectures about dangerous substances at college (diet cola) and subsequently was the one to teach us how to safely handle the real substances we might encounter. When I left for college, he handed me a note celebrating our shared history of being named after our grandmother, Lucille, who died before either of us were born: "Grandpa always said there was one major love in his life. What an honor it is to be named after his love."

He never let me take myself too seriously. He was my roommate in Hoboken my first year of teaching, before Zac and I moved in together. He fed me microwave burritos and built me a futon from IKEA as I pored over curriculum planning. He would make sure there was still a light on as I finished my lesson plan and shouted down the hall, "Night, Lon!"

I had him to thank for choosing the path of education. At nineteen, I had to declare my major at the University of Wisconsin. I had to choose between two strong programs: the school of education or the acting specialty program. It was time to decide what I wanted to become after all—a teacher or an actor—but decision-making was not my forte. What if my choice was the wrong one? Ask anyone in that stationery store in Boca Raton, Florida, in the spring of '86, and they will retell the story of a little girl who, while visiting her great-aunt and great-uncle, could not choose between a dinosaur Trapper Keeper binder and a figurine of Minnie Mouse. I think they could hear my wailing as they were lined up at the diner next door, waiting for the four o'clock dinner rush.

Lonnie knew I was spiraling. "Hey, noodge. I heard you could use some advice." Once again, he was there to wrap his arms around me. "Here's what I do. Before you go to bed, say your decision out loud. If you sleep through the night, you know you have made the right decision."

That night, before I went to bed, I whispered aloud, "I will accept the admission to the school of education. I want to be a teacher." I slept soundly through the night. Thousands of students later, I have never once regretted my decision to step into the classroom.

He reminded me that being joyful is a choice. He called the night of Jordan's diagnosis. He listened to me cry. He reminded me of my inherent strength and then made me prove I could still remember the lyrics to Sir Mix-a-Lot's "Baby Got Back." He took my anxiety, my insecurity, my wondering about the unknown, and made it feel breezy. It was his way. Being near him was like breathing in the powder bouncing off his skis as he carved through the mountain: refreshing and invigorating. I always admired this about him. Our effusive personalities allowed us both to navigate through life easily, but I was envious of his ability to approach the big stuff less encumbered.

I could have told him I needed more time with him. More picnics sharing potato chips and bad jokes. More tales of his cross-country drives. More time to practice finding his levity because, without it, I was worried life would make me hard.

I could have told him I was listening to the reverberations of his legacy. He had a loving wife, family, and true friendship. I had found the same.

I wish he knew that even now, whenever I have to decide something, I still question the air before I go to bed.

Yet I didn't tell him any of this. Instead, I said, "I love you," and he said, "Me too, noodge."

When you walk into my house, you pass through an archway of photos. I call it the "history wall," as it is filled with the people, the moments, and the settings that made Zac and I who we are and the parents we want to be. At the top is the photo of Lonnie's bar mitzvah: olive-brown suits, pink sailor dresses. As I throw the kids' backpacks down, empty the groceries, or take off my shoes, I look up and see his arms clutching my shoulders. I can hear his lingering whisper, *Leah, I got you.*

CHAPTER 42
A Prayer for Platelets

Jordan's new medication was working, and her sleep had improved. Austin was rocking a new pair of Batman orthotics and could walk downstairs without falling.

So, it was Oliver's turn. He had developed some unusual spots on his body. It was probably just the different laundry detergent, but they would not go away. The doctor at the urgent care clinic looked concerned as she examined his blood count. The second doctor she called into the room had the same countenance. I knew this expression. This wasn't my first rodeo.

In this house, it seems the only way you can get some one-on-one attention is to have an appointment with a specialist. Oliver and I took advantage of our mommy-child morning, taking a walk and eating a special breakfast, before visiting the newest doctor in our arsenal: a pediatric hematologist. I had asked Zac if I could take him; I learned my "scared but prepared" motto was more successful when I could hear the information directly. Also, I was getting more comfortable owning how much I needed some semblance of control.

Oliver and I arrived at the hematologist's building but could not find the office.

"Excuse me, we are looking for room 305," I said to two doctors walking down the hall.

"Oh yes. It is down this hall to the right. Hey, buddy." They leaned down to match Oliver's eyes. "That's a great coat you got there."

He smiled bashfully. As they turned the corner, I commented to Oliver, "They were very helpful." It was sweet how attentive they had been.

We walked into the office, and I whispered to Oliver, "Look at all the colorful hats everyone is wearing." I always appreciated a doctor's office with good air conditioning. We waited for our turn.

After his name was called, we met a very thorough doctor. We ran through the perfunctory questions and talked about Oliver's recent outbreak of "spots." Once again, my memory of the situation has decayed with fear, but I imagine it went something like:

"Yes, this petechiae rash is quite common. We will need to continue to regulate his platelets to ultimately rule out leukemia."

Silence.

"Mrs. Moore?"

"Yes, sorry. What … what was that about leukemia?"

"You were not aware we were here to talk about the potential for leukemia?"

The extra-attentive doctors after I said, "room 305." The colorful hats covering the children's heads who were receiving chemo. It was like I was watching the end of *The Usual Suspects*, where all the clues came together. My breath was choked by my paralysis.

"No. No. My son doesn't have leukemia. His sister has something, his brother … My cousin just died. We can't also have cancer. So, no, thank you."

"Okay." She smiled. "That's not quite how that works. Let's run some tests first."

"Okay," I said as I clutched Oliver. He was interested in my coat zipper. "Doctor, I just want to add, if I may, I hope I never see you again."

"Me too, Mrs. Moore. Me too."

While most of this conversation is recall, I am certain I told that nice doctor we never wanted to see her again.

We entered the next waiting room to get through another round of testing. I squeezed Oliver, as if my enveloping arms would generate more platelets in his body. I distracted him with lollipop bribes and a colorful car book and decided to have a little chat with God.

I was not one for prayers. When I was a little girl, I would say the alphabet in temple and hope that a higher power could put it together to make what was needed. I had been hearing a lot about God since Jordan's diagnosis, as many found it a comfort to explain that my family would never be given more than we could handle. This sentiment was helpful for many, but it never brought me much solace. It seemed as if we had already proven we were pretty tough. Waiting in that doctor's office, I had no more strength. I had spent years pushing aside my emotions, but this time I just needed to swim in my terror. I wish it hadn't taken something so fearful to make me realize my way of coping wasn't working.

I went off instinct. My prayer began in Hebrew with the blessing said over challah and ended with the English plea, *Please let my baby be okay.* Just in case, I tried the complete English version. *We are doing the best we can. Please keep this child healthy.*

By our fourth reading of the truck book, it was Oliver's turn to get his blood drawn. They chose his left arm, as the vein was more accessible. It was hard to contain him, because he is a small, squiggly boy, but I had carried enough car seats to clutch him tightly. His right hand escaped to stop the phlebotomist, which immediately caused the needle to impale his pointer finger. The receptionist staff came running in to see what had caused the screaming. The phlebotomist's profuse apologies were only making it worse, and I miraculously calmed my child as the needle that had pierced through his entire finger was removed.

Maybe I should try my prayers in another way. Perhaps God preferred some Shakespearean iambic pentameter.

"Ma'am, I have to tell you …" the phlebotomist began after we got Oliver's finger cleaned up.

"What?"

"I still need to take his blood. We need four more vials."

I was done. No one should have to be this durable. Seriously. I grasped this two-year-old boy in fear but smiled down at him without as much as a furrowed brow. It's the same trick I learned when Jordan was working on her receptive language. Oliver would be able to read my body language.

"After this, should we go get some ice cream?" I whispered. I couldn't stop what was happening with his blood or this clinic, but I changed the subject. It was, after all, a combo of my favorite coping mechanisms: distraction and food.

Zac and I again found ourselves on autopilot as parents. It is what happens to us when we are truly distressed. We tried to talk about Oliver, but we couldn't find the words. In fact, I don't recall us allowing ourselves to talk about the what-if. Our families checked in on us and provided as much comfort as possible. Zac and I just skated on the surface: the next appointment, the paperwork, the facts. The other two children. The doctors determined they needed to monitor Oliver's platelets for several months before making conclusive decisions. We found ourselves back on the couch, with some distracting television and treats. We had been here before.

I went to bed every night, bargaining with a higher power. My mom raised us on the concept of mitzvah points. You did a good deed and could get imaginary points to transfer to whatever you needed. It's karma, juju, kindness. I would gather all the mitzvah points in the world to keep this child safe. In the quiet, the feeling that arose was guilt. I had already spent so long worrying about Jordan and her diagnosis. I knew the fear of going into surgery and going under anesthesia, but none of that was compared to a medically fragile child. I had done my best to train myself for whatever would come next in our family, but I never bargained for this.

The next step was for the hematologist to perform a spinal tap to give us more information. I knew how much that hurt, and I didn't think I could watch my baby go through it. A brave Zac escorted a brave Oliver into the surgical room. He held Oliver's hand as the anesthesiologist placed a mask over his face, just as Zac had done for Jordan's surgery at birth and Austin's eye surgery. Zac never shared the specific details of what it was like to watch your child's induction of anesthesia, but he always exited the same, stone-faced and clutching the stuffed animal the child had selected for the procedure. I was always in the hallway, waiting for him and eating brownies. In this case, when Zac entered with Oliver's beloved Bobo, we spent time gathering materials for Bobo so he could have the same matching Band-Aids and armbands as Oliver would when he woke up.

The moment you see your child waking up from anesthesia is enough to make you want to return them to the womb. Anything to reassure them they are safe and will be fine. They clutch their juice box, with their eyes barely cracked open, so helpless and ready to be held.

When the final spinal tap came back, our pediatric hematologist and oncologist, who had now moved to our speed dial, had definitive news. It was: idiopathic thrombocytopenic purpura (ITP, for short).

Not cancer.

Although many children outgrow this diagnosis, it appeared Oliver would have this autoimmune disease for his life. He would require blood tests, and he might not be able to play contact sports, and we would need to manage the warning signs. If the platelets were too low, he would require a transfusion. This seemed unlikely.

For now, we have been teaching Oliver the secrets of carpet hockey, to keep him safe from any contact. We are grateful that if one of the three children needed to have a diagnosis that required getting blood tests so often, it is the one who does not have special sensory needs. Oliver is learning how to take ownership over his body, even at a young age. He spotted his own petechiae rash, a warning sign. He knew a spontaneous bloody nose meant we needed to rush to the emergency room to take his platelet count. He told the phlebotomist he wanted a bandage with a star drawn on it. He directed himself to the gift shop to pick out a candy treat—for everyone.

When we returned home from our latest ER visit, he went to play with his trains, happily examining his star bandage. Sometimes he is so brave, I forget he is just a little boy. On this occasion, he looked up and panicked when he didn't see me. When I came running at the sound of his shrieks, he whispered in fear, "Mommy, keep me safe."

I brought him up to his room for bedtime and hugged him fiercely. I secured Bobo in his arms and tucked in his corners a little tighter just to prove how safe he was.

It is my privilege, my obligation, my purpose to keep him safe. But this is the hardest part of motherhood: cradle to grave, managing your child's safety. How much of that was in my control? It was the same vulnerability I'd had handing a week-old Jordan to the surgeon, putting a week-old Austin into an MRI machine, and now the aftermath of thinking my toddler had leukemia. It is enough to leave me with a heart swollen from fatigue and fear.

I needed my own mom's hug. I invited her out to breakfast. We quickly fell into the melody of conversation that can only be found after thirty-six years of cultivating a relationship. The lilt of her voice, describing the upcoming holidays, was reminiscent of the bedtime stories she'd told me as a child. The concern in her forehead mirrored the gaze in 1994 when my classmates' taunting had grown excessive. And the way she twisted the napkin with her hands mirrored my own.

"I am having a hard time," I allowed myself to say, and then I spilled out the contents of my brain. She knew, of course, and she just listened.

When I look back on that moment, I see a woman grieving the recent loss of her nephew. I see a grandmother worried about the safety of her own grandchildren and the well-being of her daughter and son-in-law. But the strength of motherhood is that she didn't let me see any of that, not then. She just held me.

She would begin to try to put me back together—it was her job to keep me safe. For now, she enveloped me with her loving arms, and I allowed her to take some of the weight. It was my mom's turn to love me big.

I cannot see when the next challenge of motherhood is going to hit, but if I have learned anything, there will be more. I am grateful in these times; I can take a break from being the protector and just allow myself to be held.

CHAPTER 43

English Lesson 2—
Epic Poetry

"Midway upon the journey of our life / I found myself within a dark wood, / For the straightforward pathway had been lost." These are the opening lines of Dante Alighieri's *Inferno*. While it has been years since I've taught these lines to my students, they have always resonated with me as a profound way to capture struggle. Dante constructs his epic poem from *The Divine Comedy* as an exiled man, contemplating his life and his struggle to even produce notable writing. He developed the protagonist, Dante the Pilgrim, as a man lost in the dark woods in the middle of his life's journey. He initially saw a path leading toward hope, but it was blocked, mostly by symbolic vices. Instead, he learns, through the guide he designs for himself—Virgil—that he must travel through hell in order to get to the stars.

This was how I told Zac I wasn't feeling like myself. I, too, was lost in the "dark woods." It was the only language I could access to describe what I was feeling. I noticed it during a string of days when nothing challenging happened. It was just a typical day of parenting. Murphy's law had settled into the foundation of our home, so that when everything was fine, I didn't quite know what to do with myself. I had become so accustomed to managing the chaos that when there was no doctor to brainstorm with, no new issue to advocate for, no new transition to set up, I didn't know how to function. I just settled into autopilot. Rather than pausing to press on the pain of what we had been through, I would just turn the television volume higher. It was easier.

I had been living so intensely in flight or fright for so long, becoming tolerant of such high levels of stress, I wasn't even aware of it. In the moments of quiet, where I could begin to process some of the events that had transpired, I was terrified of the avalanche I would unfurl. So, instead of owning anything negative, I just continued to search for the positive. There was so much to be grateful for, I didn't want to squander any of my happiness. Which meant I never processed anything that was painful. When it got to the point where there was too much sadness to contain, it started to seep out of me like a wound I was purposely ignoring.

When I was able to articulate it, I found I had some company in the darkness: Zac was stranded as well. Of course he was. We knew some parents of special needs children experienced emotions like the grief cycle after a death. Maybe we had gotten stuck along the journey. Call it what you will: parenting young children, transitional disorder, functional depression. Regardless, we weren't doing great.

Finding joy had become cumbersome work, and days, weeks would pass without a glimpse of it. We knew if we didn't fight for something different, we would just be swallowed by the weight of it all. We worked to examine our triggers. Zac would get overwhelmed by the frenetic chaos of three children, and I would sink to meet him there. I was struggling to regain a sense of the person I used to be, and Zac would keep my misery company. After his long days at work, he would return to a house where I barely said a word. He would kiss my forehead and we would just wait for the day to end. We were so polite in our sorrow. Perhaps we had become codependent—or just typical tired parents.

We divided and conquered. We tried to focus on moments that were working, no matter how brief they might have been. Zac redirected his attention to help the boys, now almost three, to focus their excessive energy. Rather than throwing wooden rocking horses at each other, they could work on puzzles. LEGO blocks could be used to build a superhero castle, not just become hazardous ankle breakers on the floor. Zac spent hours teaching Oliver to kick a soccer ball and Austin to rebuild any remote control he found in the house. The boys were getting older, which meant they had a bit more focus for these activities.

I turned my attention to Jordan, age seven. After a day of school, Jordan's most preferred activity was to put on her Jasmine pajamas, place a dance skirt around her head, and hang out with herself in front of the mirror. She and her reflection had long-winded discussions that appeared to be recreating the events of her day. She asked her reflection to sign up for her imaginary YouTube page and told her dolls to "subscribe below." She placed one hand on a hip and used the other to make pronounced gestures. Her inflection mirrored that of a 1960s teenage girl sitting cross-legged and dreaming of Conrad Birdie. While an unfamiliar listener would not have understood every word, her message was always clear: she was here to have a good time. It was enjoyable to watch, even in my haze.

She reminded me of myself as a little girl. Traipsing through the house in pounds of costume jewelry, forcing my sister to listen to my original songs, I maintained the spirit of this girl well into my thirties, but my role as mother, caretaker, and special needs parent had made her a distant memory. I rarely heard myself laugh anymore and couldn't connect. No one would blame me for not contributing to the other mothers' discussion of sleepovers when I was still desperately trying to potty train my seven-year-old daughter. I tried not to harden when someone complained that the worst part of their day was "not getting to the gym," while I was still paying insurance bills from the oncologist's office. I was desperate for connection but so sensitive to these emotional triggers from parents who meant well, I ended up in a worse place than I'd started. I wasn't ready to admit that I wondered what life would have been like without children; it made me feel as if I'd failed them.

I would watch Jordan and wistfully wonder what she would have been like without developmental delays. Imagine how incredible it would be if she were this animated *and* people could understand her. I bet she would make them laugh. She inherited the performance gene from both of her parents, the world was clearly her stage; it seemed painful that only her mirror witnessed her talent.

"She could be the star of a show," I would say regretfully to Zac.

"I think she is now," Zac would respond.

He was right. Jordan was impervious to my problematic thinking. I had absorbed the societal notion that a person with a disability, especially one as pronounced as Jordan's, would prefer to be without it. This was the concept of ableism, the very issue I teach my students to examine in literature. It limited the potential of individuals with disabilities, made them disenfranchised. This was unacceptable. For society and for me. It would take me a while before I understood how to manage it. For the moment, I could just identify it.

When Jordan looked in that mirror, she was receiving a standing ovation at Carnegie Hall. She'd completed her encore at Lincoln Center. She was signing autographs at the stage door. She saw herself as a star performer—why didn't I? This was the root of my sorrow. I felt like a hypocrite. I claimed to be an advocate for my daughter but was still trying to mold her into society's definition. It was not out of my bounds as a mother to want an easy, successful life for her, but I could redefine the terms of what that looked like. Her unyielding joy was enough to unstick my feet and, like Dante, push me toward hope.

It was one thing to learn how to accept this diagnosis in my own life, but it was another to help society do the same. I needed first to give myself time to replenish my strength, reclaim my sense of self, before I was able to turn my attention outward.

While Zac and I were lost in the dark woods, we realized two things: we were not alone in there, and we'd likely be back to visit again. We had to give ourselves permission to accept that needing help is in no way failing our children; in fact, it is what we needed to become better parents. We found our Virgils and asked them to guide us to safety on our journey. We found them in therapy, other cri du chat families, a friendly face at a Special Education Parent Teacher Association (SEPTA) meeting, our encouraging family, friends, and even our own children. We consciously own the parts of our story that are tragedy but do not forget the comedy that lives there as well. We are realistic to know that not every day, month, or year will have a happy ending, but joy is out there, and we must live in a way that lets us find it. It is then we grab our Virgils, hang on, and hopefully wait to see the stars begin to emerge.

CHAPTER 44
I Really Mean It

When we were in graduate school, my husband was interviewed for a class about his relationship with me. He described it as "something built on wonderful."

That's the thing about love. Even when opposing forces attempt to shake it, if the foundation is there, it remains a constant. Our entire lives have been built on this sense of "wonderful." We captured it in our wedding bands, inscribed with the words, *I really mean it*. This was a legacy my father had initiated with my mother. He always maintained his sense of humor, so she could never be quite sure if he was pulling her leg; for all important matters, they applied the "I really mean it" rule. It was simple: you cannot lie when the words are spoken. For our marriage, the rule has become a modern ketubah of sorts, a proclamation of our vows.

We planned a trip to celebrate our ten-year wedding anniversary, recalling the first time we made "I really mean it" official. A Michael Bublé song had crooned for our first dance a decade ago: Michael Bublé had crooned out our first dance song a decade before, as he sang about how with love, we can always see things through. True to our mantra, we had planned something to look forward to, but this time was a bit more complicated. Our trip to Bermuda now served more purpose than just celebrating our anniversary. We had an unimaginable task to complete. We intertwined our inscribed rings as we let our feet dangle off the Bermuda pier. Between us sat two gray, plastic boxes. The official label on one box had faded. We had kept that box on the top of our desk for years before packing it in our carry-on. Where does one leave such a box after all?

An identical box had appeared six years later. The markings were different, but it was unmistakably the same. When the doorbell rang, the postman passed me the contents carefully, positioning the box so I could see the Cochran's Funeral Home label prominently.

The children gathered by the door, as they do anytime the bell rings. "Mommy, what's in the box?"

Aunt Amanda's remains.

"Something really special. We are going to leave it right here; please don't touch it."

Zac had rushed to Texas when we learned she was in a coma. We took solace knowing her passing was without pain, but the pain it caused in our home was staggering. Her heart just couldn't take any more. Neither could ours. Her funeral was perfectly her; just enough sparkle.

We knew we would release the two boxes together. We decided to keep them safe until we could make it to the crystal waters of Bermuda.

Our first time walking the streets of Bermuda, just after our engagement, Jacquie and Amanda could not get enough ornate jewelry, decorative plates, and humorous T-shirts. "Perhaps you should wear these on your honeymoon," Amanda teased me.

Ten years later, Zac and I walked alone, carrying only our diaper bag. The typical wipes and extra snacks for the kids, who were not with us, were replaced by both boxes. They were surprisingly light despite their heaviness. We carried them with us for the entire day, through the streets of Hamilton, down Church Street, and into the local shops. It felt comforting to have the boxes with us, as if we weren't alone. I picked up a plate. I had seen this before. I think I put it in the donation pile when we cleaned out the house in Houston. I tightened the straps on my backpack and exited the store.

We searched until we found the perfect place. We had not planned the particulars, just a peaceful spot near the water. We let our feet dangle over the edge and placed the contents of our diaper bag delicately on our laps. Two boxes. We remained silent and together we turned them over. The dust gently mixed together in the eastern wind, as if holding hands. The ashes collected at the surface of the water and quickly dissipated. Mother and daughter, together forever at rest.

"Aunt Amanda died," we had told the kids after careful discussion with the family trainer, who said that we needed to use as direct but sensitive language as possible. Jordan would not understand euphemisms. "We cannot see her, but she will live in our hearts."

"Grandma Jacquie lives in our hearts. Maybe she will see her there," Jordan suggested. She smiled. She liked that idea. I did too.

On that clear Bermuda morning, I grabbed Zac's hand. I would hold him on this pier, back in New York, and through our next obstacle. We are "something built on wonderful." We sat silently until there was nothing more to say. We threw the boxes away and hopped a bus to the next island.

This is what we do: we fight for balance. We spread ashes in the morning and win cruise bingo at night. We desperately miss our children and then revel in sleeping in past 4:00 a.m. We shed tears of sorrow over lunch and then dominate show tune trivia in the evening.

We are continually reminded it is human to feel the opposing forces of life around you.

There is a place for sorrow in a house of joy.

There is a way to not lose yourself trying.

I really mean it.

PART III
"LADYBUG WARRIORS"

*"Do the best you can until you know better.
Then when you know better, do better."*
                                    —MAYA ANGELOU

It Just Takes One

 It started in my basement.

The stuffed animals would sit on top of the Ping-Pong table, waiting to find out if they had passed the spelling quiz. Beary could never spell "because" correctly and would have to stay after school to get some more help. When Humpy the Dinosaur said something mean to Beary, I would stop class to explain why his words were hurtful. It was my classroom. My rules.

The rules should have gotten more complicated when the stuffed animals turned into real teenagers, but they remained true. What we say matters. What we do matters. In my classroom, I can shape the words we use to lead with kindness. My students discuss the historical roots of discriminatory words and learn how to become upstanders to eradicate them from their communities. However, in my mothering world, this discussion becomes more complicated, more personal. In some cases, discrimination is rampant, or many ignore opportunities to be allies. But, among the noise, there are those who have become the "ladybug warriors." This term, coined by children's author Dianna Hutts Aston in *A Beetle Is Shy*, is used to describe people among us who, like ladybugs, eat away at negativity, quietly and thoughtfully, to let what is beautiful thrive. These are the people who are ready to love big, and they don't care who is listening.

My mentor at school often reminded the students that when you hear something infuriating or uncomfortable, the body demonstrates physical signs: a pit in your stomach, blushing, sweaty palms; however, we experience the same physiological responses when we stand up for something we believe in. The adrenaline rush of advocacy. Therefore, if you are going to be red in the face either way, why not try to stand up for what you believe? As Maggie Kuhn boldly stated, "Speak your mind even if your voice shakes." But you learn, when it is about your child, you won't even flinch.

CHAPTER 45
The Sunflower

When the boys were two, they started planting a garden. This was their special activity with BaBa while Mommy and Daddy were at work. They would plant seeds, water their soil, and watch their flowers bloom. Austin's flower was the envy of the family. It grew taller than he was and, despite all the other flowers wilting, continued to extend high into the air.

"Hi, flower," he would chime before entering the house every day. He would extend his arms around it, careful not to break it, and give it a "flower hug."

The morning the roofers came to repair our roof, his flower was trampled.

I came home to a decapitated flower and a wilting Austin. "Mommy, I need tape. My flower is broken."

When the roofer came to pick up the final payment, Austin pushed his way through the doorway and said, "You broke my flower."

I redirected him; this was, after all, a house of kindness. "Austin, thank the kind man for giving you a roof over your head—literally."

"No. My flower is broken."

I apologetically smiled at the man, thanked him for the countless hours precariously standing on top of my roof, and closed the door.

I worked on consoling Austin. We were almost at the point where we needed to sit shiva for the flower, he was so upset. He would enter the house, look at his empty flower box, and say, "No flower. No flower hug." It was adorably heartbreaking.

Two days later a box arrived from Amazon, addressed to Austin. He pulled out a small container and a note: *I am sorry your flower was broken. Here is a new one for you.* In his hands was a brand-new sunflower kit.

We'd never seen him so happy.

Zac called the roofing company.

"We don't know what you are talking about," they said, "but that is a very sweet gesture."

I called my sister. My parents. My in-laws. The neighbors.

Nope, they all said. *What a sweet gesture.*

The sunflower mystery revealed two facts: I clearly tell a lot of people about the daily events in our lives, and we have quite a support system. There was someone in our lives so kind that when they heard about the love saga of a boy and his flower, they took a few minutes from their day to brighten his.

I had spent the last seven years in such an insular state. It was necessary to do so. I practically earned a PhD in parenting with a new language to learn, hours of training, workshops, and practical experience. Add in mourning, and it was all I could do to not turn to stone. I needed to harden to learn how to survive a perpetually heightened state in case I needed to respond to a crisis. I was prepared. Sturdy. Anchored. My marriage and sanity had survived final exams, and I was ready to graduate. However, to establish my own roots, I'd neglected some of my responsibilities to the people in my life for almost a decade. I was ready to reconnect to the outside world, but I wasn't sure what was waiting for me.

As it turns out, a lush support system. With each call or text to another person—"Do you know anything about a mysterious sunflower?"—I realized just how vast our community was. This incredible team of neighbors, coworkers, family, and friends had been here all along. When I discovered my mystery benefactor, my incredible friend and coworker who had been keeping me afloat for years, I thanked her. I was grateful, not just for her thoughtfulness, but also for reminding me of the extensive team we had around us. It gave me the strength I needed to do some of the bigger work.

Austin's new sunflower bloomed safely in the comfort of our kitchen. "Hi, flower!" he shouted as he ran past it to chase Oliver. It served as a beautiful reminder that we all have more than one chance to bloom.

CHAPTER 46
A Lesson in Kindness

Austin told me he was learning how to "fill his bucket" at school. His teacher was helping the preschool students learn how to behave in a way that would make someone else's day. When I put cooked carrots on his plate, Oliver shared his race car, or Zac tucked him in, Austin would reveal his sweet dimples and coo, "You fill my bucket." He overgeneralized this idea and plopped underneath Zac, who was doing push-ups, shouting, "Yeah, Daddy. You fill my bucket," with each rep. Austin could become a bucket ambassador for our family, as we were meeting many people who could have used a review of this childhood lesson.

There was the mother at the neighborhood playground who shushed her daughter when she pointed to Jordan's knee-high orthotics and asked, "What's wrong with her legs?" Then she embarrassingly looked in our direction and moved her daughter to the other side of the park while I silently watched them leave.

Or the man at the community center watching Jordan's class performance, asking his friend, "Are these kids retarded or something?" I didn't say a word.

Or the receptionist at the sports complex who told me, "Some instructors don't want to work with kids like her, if you know what I mean." Still, nothing.

I was receiving these discriminatory comments and yet remained silent. I teach advocacy in my classroom, inspiring young people to stand up for the marginalized groups we read about in literature, to avoid the use of derogatory language. Yet in my backyard, I was nonconfrontational. I was raising a child who needed someone to reposition obstacles for her. If I couldn't risk a little awkwardness to empower her voice, who was going to?

I found insight with Nigerian author Chimamanda Ngozi Adichie's talk, "The Danger of a Single Story." She explains, "The single story creates stereotypes, and the problem with stereotypes is not that they are untrue, but they are incomplete. They make one story become the only story." In this case, the misrepresentation of individuals with disabilities.

I recalled the days after Jordan's diagnosis. The sympathy cards, the tears, the fear. So many of us had heard only the negative stories, me included; we had a single story of what it meant to raise a child with special needs. There was a message that a diagnosis was something that needed to be mourned and, with enough resources, could be fixed. These children are individuals who burden their families, tax the resources of the health-care system. Their differences somehow make them worthy of alienation. This way of thinking is archaic and problematic.

When I reflected on the previous years of Jordan's life, I noticed how I, too, was guilty of these implicit biases. I am her mother. I am her biggest advocate and love her ferociously, yet I was absorbing the power of the societal whispers swirling beneath our daily lives: *she is not able.*

I was listening when my sister, like a proud aunt, questioned Jordan's future profession and I frowned and said, "She will be living with us."

I was listening when I let Jordan get away with her negative behaviors because I didn't think she could fix them.

I was listening when I thought with enough resources, therapies, and appointments, I could love the disability out of my child.

I was listening every time I stayed silent.

This misguided representation of ability is a story rooted in the historical oppression of the eugenics movement, a period when individuals with cognitive, physical, and emotional disabilities were abandoned, sterilized, and filling our institutions. With every depiction of individuals with disabilities seen as pitiable, an object of violence or ridicule, nonsexual, or unable to participate fully in society, the media perpetuates this misrepresentation.[1] This is the reason why individuals with physical and cognitive disabilities were on the periphery of my life. This is the reason the word *normal* should be avoided. This is the root of an ableist society. This discrimination of people with cognitive, intellectual, or emotional disabilities, whether visible or invisible, needs to change.

And it is starting. We smile with *Speechless*'s JJ DiMeo rather than mourn Steinbeck's Lennie Small. We replace stares with introductions. We greet Julia from *Sesame Street* into our homes, and not just Tiny Tim. We see adaptive clothing lines on the shelves and new emoji options for our phones. We make room to include more stories. All the stories.

Including ours.

It took me a few years, but I have learned how to raise my voice.

I hadn't intended to unleash this new perspective at my daughter's dance recital, but when Zac and I watched our beautiful little ballerina, proudly wearing her cotton-candy tutu, with her round belly jutting out, how could I not speak up for her?

Four ballerinas lined up perfectly in formation while my hilarious breath of fresh air was visiting her favorite friend: her reflection. Jordan was the only child who was not neurotypical in the class. The teacher smiled a brave, knowing look in my direction as she redirected Jordan

---

1 "Discrimination: Disabled People and the Media," *Contact*, no. 70 (Winter 1991): 45–48.

to her spot. The music started and the smile on Jordan's face could not be contained. She began to dance! Zac's hand found mine while we tearfully giggled. She bobbed up and down. She swayed to the side. She shouted at the top of her lungs. She was living her best self.

The rest of the girls were still only going through their initial positions. Their feet had not left their designated shape, and the only movement they had made was between first and second position. Our bellowing ballerina was following her own internal beat.

"Ugh. That child is so distracting. My Rebecca cannot concentrate," I heard the woman next to me hiss.

A fire flashed throughout my entire body. I turned my head, calculating to make eye contact with this mother. My snarling fangs, my extended claws—I had morphed into Mama Bear. No one would talk about my baby that way. But I was not going to ruin Jordan's moment. I would address this when I had a moment to collect myself. I breathed down the anger and only focused on my blissful ballerina. This woman would not ruin this experience for us.

Jordan radiated joy on the stage. She clapped for the other girls during their individual moments and listened as best she could to the teacher's directions. She was still bowing when we buckled her car seat.

After I put her fatigued body to bed, I thought about my choices. The mother in me tried to empathize with this woman. She wanted her Rebecca to have the best experience possible, and perhaps my child was interrupting that. Yet this was a beginner ballet class, and no one made an audible comment about the adorable redhead picking her nose during the finale. I could just let it go—it was just one woman, and it was not my responsibility to educate her on kindness. Or was it? I couldn't let the "ugh" in her comment go. It was the disdain in her voice that got to me. My child deserved the same compassion and empathy as everyone else. I had to say something. I just didn't know how.

Like most people flexing a new muscle, first I practiced what I wanted to say with a friend. When I finished explaining the situation, it turned out that my friend had a mutual friend with the woman in the dance class. This started a chain reaction that meant the woman in dance class approached me.

While I had imagined what I would say to her, when she confronted me after dance class the next week, my response was more muddled than my rehearsal.

"I think there was a misunderstanding about what happened with your daughter in dance class," she started.

My face turned red instantly. It was one of my least favorite qualities, how intensely I blushed, especially when the soccer players in my ninth-grade ceramics class had learned how quickly it would appear. It's always been a bit of a tell that I wish I could overcome.

"Yes, I was going to say something about that," I responded.

"I was explaining to my child that your daughter still wears diapers. She asked."

"Oh." (That too.) "What I actually wanted to talk to you about was the comment you made while she was dancing at the recital last week. You scoffed and said Jordan was distracting. I think you should know how hurtful the comment was. She wasn't supposed to walk, so you can imagine how it feels as her parents to see her up there dancing. What you saw as distracting is the way she communicates with the world." I used my teacher voice. Stern and calm.

"You must have misunderstood. I said my daughter was distracted, not that your daughter was distracting."

This wasn't going to be easy.

"We don't have to get into the details of semantics. I would just like you to understand how your comment was hurtful toward my family, and to consider your future ones."

"Of course. I'm glad your daughter is in the class. I love diversity."

Me: ...

I excused myself. There was nothing more to say. I kept my distance for the remaining classes but did not engage any further. That conversation had been painful, stressful, and empowering. It was my first time standing up for my child, and I vowed to handle it very differently next time. I wouldn't wait for someone to come to me, I wouldn't let the conversation finish so quickly, and I wouldn't feel like I needed to rehearse what I wanted to say. Jordan's presence was not problematic, and I would never let anyone state otherwise.

That woman still makes me feel angry. I can no longer remember her name or see her face. I can only hear the "ugh." That was all I'd needed to propel me onto the long road I wanted to travel as an advocate. I just needed to know I had it in me.

CHAPTER 47
Throw Your Oxygen Mask
Out the Window

"I really don't know how you do it all."

This is the most common observation I hear as a mother when I am out in the world. I am hoping it is said so often because three loud children are a noticeable handful, and not because one of those children has obvious differences. Because then the comment becomes less of a compliment and more of a placeholder for, "I couldn't do what you do and I'm fortunate I don't have to." Because, if it is the latter, my child with a disability is reduced to just her disability, and that is not okay. Since I don't have enough information to know if I am being praised or pitied, I just politely smile and leave.

My smile is always genuine. It's been sort of my trademark move since the early eighties. It's how I earned the coveted lead in *Snow White* at Willow Lake Day Camp and why my photo is located next to "Friendliest" in the 1999 Roxbury High School Yearbook. Smiling is just the natural position of my face. Maybe it balances out my untamable curly hair, but it is also my armor for when I don't know what to say. Spend enough years in clown camp and you, too, can learn to plaster on a convincing smile.

The observation of handling "it all" is a strange type of compliment, as if saying, "I notice you have a lot to manage and I'm impressed none of your children have been impaled." Yet the notion of "it all" suggests there is a finite number of things to learn as a parent, which adds unnecessary pressure to an already beautifully burdensome situation.

When you become a special needs parent, they have a speech to prepare you for this type of pressure: put your oxygen mask on first. It's popular with many caretakers, therapists, and parents. The message is important: before you can take care of anyone else, you need to first take care of yourself. The problem is, I found a loophole. I found a way to survive with catch breaths, shallow sips of air, like I'd use in singing. Somewhere in the middle of working full-time, supporting Jordan, exploring Austin's medical needs, and remembering Oliver was not yet old enough to take care of himself, I found that the way to get "it all" done was to take quick sips of breath. By deeming full breaths superfluous, I could get just enough oxygen during my lunch break (while I made phone calls to the insurance company). Anything that required true oxygen, or the aspects of life usually found higher on Maslow's hierarchy of needs, was a luxury I did not have time for. If I had stopped to consider how close I was to asphyxiation, I'd have been paralyzed by it all. I had to remain alert, prepared in my ready stance, like I'd done as a child playing catch with my dad. If I didn't stop moving, I could adjust, ready for whatever direction the ball would fly, jumping for a fly ball or ducking for a grounder.

I got used to living in this perpetual flight response. If I never let my defenses down, I didn't have time to be vulnerable. I even became proud of my new identity. I was the woman who got things done. Never mind my coworkers were concerned at the pace I moved, or that Zac and I did not have one conversation beyond necessity. I had a busy life, and there was no time to figure out how to do it. I just did it.

Holding my breath became my mom badge of honor, not something I was concerned about. I ignored the nagging pressure in my chest and swallowed the stress. I convinced myself I was an excellent multitasker and that if I worked fast enough, I would never have to admit I was on my way to suffocating. And if I did suffocate, I just relied on those acting skills and hoped my smile could cover it.

The only space where I didn't flounder was inside my classroom. It was a true separation from my home life and a way to remember the person I had been *before*. When the students in my ninth-grade English class were working on a personal narrative unit, I wanted to model the assignment.

So one evening, after my kids had finally gone to bed, I wearily sat down at the computer—frustrated that I had added more to my plate—and tried to write. I started typing, and the beginning of this memoir poured out of me.

Then the stories kept coming. With each story, I found a way to put into words what I had only been swallowing in silence. It was how I reconciled the tension that Jordan may never use words. It was how I assuaged my guilt about not attending another birthday party because the rigorous therapy schedule didn't give us time. It was how I had organized myself after the twins were born and then privately handled the medical scares. The more the words showed up on paper, the less I carried the weight of them. Writing replaced my forced smile with an authentic one.

I replaced eating chocolate in the bathroom with writing on the laptop in the basement. Zac patiently put Jordan to bed as I released a sentence from my brain. I jotted down notes as Oliver rested on my head to watch *PAW Patrol*. I held a sleeping Austin while I dictated ideas into my phone. Now when I needed to redirect a sobbing Jordan, I focused on how I was doing it, no longer wishing to escape. Writing was forcing me to become present in the lives of my children, paying attention to their wants, frustrations, and joys.

I've always had the sensation to write; I just never knew what subject to choose. In middle school, I wrote a children's book about a penny who had an unfulfilled life, and then spent the rest of the decade writing unrequited love poems. A short story in college was based on the true tale of inadvertently punching a squirrel in the face while I was throwing away my lunch (spoiler: the squirrel community came for revenge). I naturally became more sophisticated in the early 2000s and wrote some more humiliating sonnets. The only fiction I seemed to create was in my dreams, and I couldn't recall enough of it in my waking hours to write it down. My life didn't feel interesting enough to spark the next great manuscript.

The circumstances of my life shifted my view of writing. I am learning to live in a way that allows me to pay attention to where my stories are hiding. That's the thing about living your stories: they are everywhere. On paper, I can construct what I wish I had said to the comments I received in public. On paper, I can make sure I speak the truth. On paper, I have time.

The more I write, the more I notice. Writing has grounded me. It is no longer just about me and processing my challenges. It has become a way to amplify my daughter's voice, so she is not defined by her diagnosis. I listen to disability rights activist James Charlton who states, "nothing about us without us." I do not have a disability and I cannot speak for my daughter. It would be problematic for me to do so. I am, however, in a position to share her voice when I can. (It is the reason the first words in this book belong to her.) I can do my part as her mother to fight for more stories to be heard.

I will continue writing until the people who stare at her orthotics on the playground learn to come over and say "hello."

I will continue writing until children are not regarded with polite invisibility, but receive genuine invitations to sit at the lunch table.

I will continue writing until a community that has been relegated to the sidelines for too long becomes mainstream.

So, here's my response to the people who say, "I really don't know how you do it all."

You are reading my attempt to figure it out.

CHAPTER 48

A Word of Wisdom from a Special Needs Dad

"Hey." I collapse onto Zac at the end of another long day. The children are finally asleep. "Are you doing okay?"

"Yeah. You know."

"Yeah."

The silence is filled with the echoes of our day: negotiating wearing shoes, fighting to brush teeth, and having phone calls with specialists. It is always a decision whether we need to debrief the day or just let it dissipate into the quiet. This evening, I need to get out of my own head and hear Zac's perspective about this crazy crew.

"How are you really doing?" I ask.

"Well, Daniel Tiger has lied to us."

I love talking to my husband.

A summary of his *Daniel Tiger* rant. In every episode, Daniel's difficulty is dealt with by a simple explanation of feelings, a redirection, and an occasional song, and the problem is solved. Zac is right. The "Grown-ups Come Back Song" does not soothe a screaming Austin when we leave for work in the morning. But it stays in my ear for the rest of the day.

"The reality is, the experts can tell us what to expect, but no one is really going to tell us how to handle Jordan," Zac told me. "We have to be her experts. We never know when she is going to snap. Our house is a state of extremes. It's hard not to let what is difficult define the rest of the day. It's hard to figure out how not to entirely sink."

"I know." I grab the Dallas Cowboys blanket his mom made us for Christmas years ago and pull it over the two of us.

"Do you want to try to figure it out now? Or do you want to just watch *Schitt's Creek* and we can figure it out tomorrow?"

"Pass me the remote."

CHAPTER 49
The Makeup Artist

"Well, that's not great."

"What, honey?" Zac calls from the bedroom.

"Oh, nothing." I did not realize I'd said that aloud.

I catch a glimpse of my reflection in the mirror as I attempt to get dressed for work. I am something out of a Rubens painting. I am going to throw in some contacts, dab on lip balm, and call it a day. The years of emotional eating have taken a toll on me. I know I have to work on this, but I cannot replace that behavior until I find something else that will work. I once read that emotional eating provides a log in the middle of a fast-moving river. It gives you something to hold on to in order to stay afloat, but if you don't replace the log, you will drown.

I pull my hair in a ponytail that somehow manages to look worse than my curly-haired bedhead, and I take a step back.

Jordan looks up from her tablet and calls to me. "Mommy, you look beautiful."

That's a nice compliment to take in. I know I am not living in the golden ages of my body, but I cannot forget what I have asked it to do. Together, we have spent hundreds of hours sitting in a classroom, learning how to teach, and then thousands of hours on our feet proving we can. We carried three babies to full term—two simultaneously—

and then became their human grocery store. These forearms lugged car seats, these legs propelled the human airplane game, and this back survived sleeping in rocking chairs. This body has taken on the emotional burden of a life filled with unplanned detours and can still bounce out (or fall out) of bed in the morning to start all over again.

When I walk down any crowded street, I find myself noticing the features on people I think are beautiful. A smile. Radiant skin. Great hair. It is something I have always done. I like to imagine I'm finding something in that person that they might not always see in themselves. Yet I often don't extend this kindness to myself. I have succumbed to the societal pressures that the media has perpetuated for every caregiver. In the middle of advocating for your child, going to work, and making lunches, a successful mom is always put together. The signs of fatigue are not evident if your shoes match your well-laundered shirt. I could never quite achieve this image, and despite having a lot of successes as a parent, I left many spaces feeling like I'd missed something because I wasn't looking the way I had hoped I would.

Luckily, I had a stylist at home who didn't care about societal pressures and had inherited my ability to recognize people's inner beauty.

"Mommy. You look beautiful today. Let's add some makeup."

She has an unorthodox manner, but I find she does the best work. She lays out all her materials in a circle surrounding her feet. Then she offers me a round of Rock, Paper, Scissors to see which item we will be starting with: lips, cheeks, eyes? From what I can discern, there are no guidelines for this, as her system changes daily and she often cheats to put her scissors out, long after my paper has presented itself. She will then close her eyes, choose her first cosmetic, and begin.

She starts by telling her viewers the name of the item and where she will be applying it. I cannot see these viewers, but I can tell from her reaction that there are many of them there. Perhaps they are on the other side of the mirror, or just in her own imagination, but when I ask her to whom she speaks, she says, "My YouTube fans, obviously. Let's continue."

She takes a blush brush to my eyeball. She pounds it several times before licking the brush and then putting it into her own eyeball. Her technique is a bit unusual. Perhaps she was trained in Paris. Most of her makeup is made of felt, so despite the shellacking she is doing, the majority of her artistry is undetectable to the human eye. She will then move toward her favorite—the lipsticks. These are real: glossy lip balms, cartoon-shaped lip glosses, and some glue sticks she has stolen from the art supplies. She holds them to my face, smiles passionately into my eyes, and then applies seven layers of each on her own face. She knows that lipstick is not just for the lips, but makes a great foundation, eye shadow, and sometimes toothpaste.

When she is really inspired, she will ignore me completely and look at herself in the mirror. She will blow a kiss to herself, compliment her reflection, and begin to apply lipstick to the inside of her eyebrows. "You have fashion, darling," she says to her reflection in her best Rarity voice from *My Little Pony*.

She offers touch-ups while I am asleep. On the occasion I collapse onto the couch, I will wake up with a face full of mascara. Real mascara that she has apparently stolen from the medicine cabinet, despite the child safety locks. I am grateful for her commitment to her craft, as I will be ready for an impromptu filming of *Lord of the Flies*, if ever needed.

Her passion for the art form is unparalleled. Her schedule is very booked, with the YouTube channel and all, but if you also need a bit of an ego boost and don't mind getting a blush brush shoved inside your ear, please reach out to make an appointment. It's good for one's self-esteem.

CHAPTER 50
Details Matter

I was a sophomore in college in 2001, vigorously punching what seemed like forty-seven numbers into my landline phone to connect Madison, Wisconsin to Bondoukou, Côte d'Ivoire. I had no more than four minutes to talk to Rachel, currently in her eighth month as a member of the Peace Corps. Up to this point, our conversations had been exchanges via a 1980s dictation machine that captured the trials and tribulations of my second year at the university. I carried the tape everywhere, transcribing the details of my lunch, whispering through a lecture on African studies, citing concern about my outfits. I eagerly awaited her responses describing the HIV education workshops she led in French, the impact she was making, the new culture she was learning.

To be without the guidance of my sister was truly unfamiliar. Her companionship had been the constant comfort of my childhood. When I finally heard her voice crackle, "How are you?" on the line, I didn't want to tell her anything I had prepared to say. It didn't matter how I was; I only wanted to hear what she was experiencing in Africa. Nothing I was doing could have been as important as her meaningful work. My hometown had even spread the rumor that she had rescued children from a fire (not true). My upcoming midterm or dorm dinner seemed truly inconsequential.

However, my wise sister took three of those precious minutes to remind me it was all relative. What was happening in my world was just as important to me as what was happening in her world. We also didn't always have to talk about the serious details; we could just share something funny that had happened. I had been subconsciously weighing what was worthy of being said. That's no fun for anyone. It leaves conversations stale and people unfulfilled. With my one remaining minute, I gave a detailed description of the popcorn chicken and side salad the dorm was serving for dinner and my desire for fries.

I often think about this as a parent. Many conversations with friends have started with them saying, "I'm sure it is harder at your house, but …" before disclosing something stressful happening to them. They did not want to burden me with the trivial details of their lives or something truly lovely that had happened. There was a misconception that people did not want to talk about their incredible savings at TJ Maxx if I'd spent my day studying the best treatment plan for seizures. Yet that was exactly what I was in the mood to hear. You have a strange neighbor who wanted to feed your dog cookies? I want to hear about it. You have a meme of a lady celebrating her Target purchases? Send it over.

Despite the inherent community, navigating parenthood is rather lonely. We are all just looking for someone else to sit with us, validate our feelings, and help us move forward. Feeling safe in a community of empathy is what each of us deserves. In her book *Dare to Lead*, Brené Brown asserts, "Empathy is not connecting to an experience. It is connecting to the emotions that underpin an experience." There is no one who can share our exact experiences, but the connection we can feel when we share our stories begins to form a community I think so many parents are looking for. Too many times, after being with a group of friends, we realize that we haven't really said anything at all. Every social occasion is not the time for deep, emotive chats, but it is important to make sure we set up a community where it is available when needed. It takes courage to honestly answer the question, "How are you?" and to not censor ourselves along the way, to trust that someone is open to listening.

I love stories. Silly, serious, mundane, moving. We owe it to ourselves to celebrate them.

I'll start.

I found one of my sons, age four, sobbing in the corner, holding a soccer ball. Since I wasn't able to get permission to use this story, I will keep their name protected. When I asked him why he was so sad, he turned to me with the most devastated eyes. "Mommy, I am worried that your tushy is lonely."

"Excuse me?" (And you can't laugh. You can never laugh when they are so earnest.)

"My tushy talks to my penis, but your tushy doesn't have anyone to talk to," he managed to get out before he burst into uncontrollable, hysterical sobs.

"Honey, I promise you my tushy is not lonely." It took all my restraint not to ask him what his tushy and penis discussed.

"But how do you know?" I had never seen him cry this hard.

"I promise. Mommies know these things. Would you like an ice pop?" (It's my only move these days.)

"Yes. Can we call Aunt Rachel?"

"You want to make sure her tushy isn't lonely too?"

He nodded.

We snuggled on the couch with our ice pop and got Aunt Rachel on the phone. We interrupted the busiest time of her day, feeding my three nieces, to ask about the status of her derriere. He didn't get off the phone until he was certain she was just fine. She patiently listened, as all "ladybug warriors" do. After all, when you tell a story, the details matter.

CHAPTER 51
"Corner of the Sky"

I knew having children would mean the loss of time and money. Not just because Jordan had a habit of ripping twenty-dollar bills in half, but because those are the facts of parenthood. What I hadn't planned on losing was music. I also didn't realize how much I'd needed it until I was surrounded by silence.

I think in lyrics. First, they were my mother's lullabies, then my parents' records, and eventually every song by Bon Jovi (it was the eighties in New Jersey). When I was five, my parents recognized my interest and took us to see *Into the Woods* on Broadway. Bernadette Peters opened her mouth and I turned to my sister and said, "She has hair like us," and then didn't breathe for the next two hours.

When I listened to music, time did not exist. I began composing my own terrible songs with original titles: "Seasons," "Friendship," and "Different People" (in that one, I just listed all the different people I had ever heard of). Carole King I wasn't, but my parents were big fans.

When no one was home, I would blast the record of *Pippin* and perform show tunes for my fireplace. I would use my mother's work line to call the house phone, wait for the answering machine to pick up, belt "Happy Birthday" into the recording, and then erase the evidence before anyone came home. I trained myself to use music to express what I was feeling. There was nothing a good lyric and melody couldn't fix. It was my form of self-care.

I carried music as the backdrop for all my life's experiences. My Fisher-Price Pocket Rockers became a Sony Walkman. The Discman CD player took over and I learned how to walk without making the CD skip. By the time I fell in love with Zac, my headphones had become attached to an MP3 player loaded with hundreds of cheesy love songs and Broadway ballads. I was in heaven.

The music left so quietly; I didn't realize until there was silence. First, Jordan wouldn't settle with a lullaby; in fact, it made her more agitated. So I would rest her on my shoulder, rock her back and forth, sing a tune in my head, and just breathe with her until she fell asleep. In the car, we noticed the radio made her cry, so we turned it off. There was no need to add more crying into an infant's life. If we hummed in the house or sang a small tune, she would swat at us to stop. Eventually, when her words came in, she would boldly shout, "No sing, Mama!"

Jordan grew and clearly expressed a flair for the dramatics, something she'd inherited from her two theatrical parents. Yet her strong aversion to music and singing remains in most situations. She is never bothered in dance class or during an occasional dance party at the house, so we keep trying to expand her tolerance. On most occasions, though, she holds her ears as if the sound is hurting her and screams until it stops. As we continue to expand having music in our home, we work within her tolerance. We replaced her lullabies with character impression games and save the evening songs for just her brothers. I am currently trying to indoctrinate my boys in learning the groundbreaking lyrics to my hit song "Friendship"—"When two people are very close, they're friends / they have friendship," it was such a hit in college—instead of reading bedtime stories. So far, they are unimpressed.

I am still learning how to layer music back into my life. I sneak in opportunities to listen or hum a tune in my head while alone and grading papers, but those interactions are not as soothing so the music is not cathartic. I crave a long car ride so I can practice my *Hamilton* lyrics like the best of them. I take walks and listen on my phone, choosing the perfect melody to match my mood. It is a momentary fix.

Sometimes, when Jordan is dancing in front of the mirror, I catch her humming to herself. She hears music; it just lives safely inside her head. I sit as close as possible, without her noticing, so I can listen and be comforted by the sound of her music.

CHAPTER 52
Empathy Spotters

In college I studied the concept of proxemics, an analysis of humans' use of space and the impact of nonverbal communication on behavior and communication. It is a sophisticated version of people-watching. My roommate thought I was psychic, but I was just observant. It did, however, allow me to help my friend identify who had a crush on him, and it was very entertaining at the airport. I mostly relied on this study of nonverbal communication to discover my surrounding "ladybug warriors."

When I heard the term, I wanted to become one of those warriors. I had spent the past three decades of my life helping people, as was the foundation of my childhood, but I hadn't always been as aware of the impact. My first opportunity as a special needs mother occurred while I was reading a book by a community pool. The twins, six months old, were blissfully asleep in the shade and Jordan was safely swimming with my husband. I was, in fact, relaxed.

I looked up when I heard laughter coming from the baby pool five feet in front of me. A teenage girl with Down syndrome had gone under the Do Not Enter sign and was splashing in the center of the water. She was laughing vibrantly and cooling her face from the hot sun. I could see her mother in the distance, running toward her from the other side of the pool. I gently stepped forward and used all the techniques I had learned as Jordan's mother to transition this young lady into a safer space. Her mother arrived in record time, as we do, and as if reading from the same script I was using, transitioned her to successfully leave the pool. The mother smiled graciously at me and left.

It was a calm scene. The girl was safe. The mother was polite. I felt helpful. She had no way of knowing I spoke the same language. It didn't matter how or why I had helped; the fact was, I was just there to help when needed.

I learned to recognize my own "ladybug warriors" with a knowing smile. They were the strangers in my life who held open the door a little longer or made small talk with my family despite their heavy groceries. There were people out there who led with kindness. They existed for all individuals but became extra helpful when working with a non-neurotypical child. These warriors did not have to have direct experience with a child with special needs to wear the badge. They were simply cultivating a world where piteous smiles were replaced with compassionate ones. When I walked around, I could hear a gentle symphony humming beneath the surface, with the "ladybug warriors" as the steady conductor.

I never knew when I would find this empathy, but it helped me to carry my weight to know that for each library, grocery store, or park, there was an orchestra of siblings, grandparents, teachers, and neighbors who got it too.

Thankfully, I found one on our first flight to Texas as a family of five. It was the same trip the airline decided to separate our seats. "We have Jordan in row one, Austin and Oliver in row seven with Zac, and Leah in row fifteen," the desk attendant informed us.

"Yeah, I don't think we are going to want to do that," I giggled, although a flight without children sounded like a dream.

They rearranged us quickly with three seats, buttressed by the wall of the bathroom, and two directly in front. Across the aisle, I smiled to a family who must have responded to an ad in central casting called "calm and friendly travelers who help frazzled families." The mother's return smile was clear: ladybug warrior. I felt more comfortable already.

It was only twenty minutes into the flight when the mother leaned across and quietly said, "I just came from a visit with my granddaughter, Laila, and I miss her already. Might I be able to hold one of your boys to give you a hand?"

I eagerly threw the weight of my son across the aisle, probably too eagerly. He didn't even look back at me. He stuck his finger into her nose and giggled as she played peekaboo. Her son showed him colorful lights on his cell phone.

This kindness allowed me ten minutes.

I stood up to see Zac, one seat in front of me, sleeping peacefully with a sleeping baby on his face. Of course, on the tarmac when we quickly played "split the twins," I had chosen the one that wanted my face to be a trampoline instead of a Sleep Number bed. But one sleeping baby meant 33 percent less to worry about, so I was too happy to be jealous. I coaxed my daughter into the bathroom, rather a torture chamber for a child with sensory needs. The walls were too close, the toilet flushed too loudly, and there was no possible way to change the diaper of a five-year-old girl. I also used the restroom, despite not having to go, because I knew this would be my only opportunity. I made a mental note not to drink or eat again for the remaining four hours. We held our fingers over our ears, dried our hands with the wind tunnel, and practically fell into the drink cart.

We made it back to our seats.

"Mama." The son on Zac's lap had woken up and wanted to join my row. He saw his brother sitting on the lap of his new friend and wanted to sit with him. My seat neighbor happily grinned and held her arms out wider. Now she had a blubbery baby on either thigh, wrapping their fingers around her colorful hijab, and trying to steal her son's cell phone. I tried to move her soda from the cascading baby drool, but she joyfully shooed my hand away.

"Thank you for letting me play with them. They are adorable."

"This is Austin and Oliver. They seem to like you too. Thank you for helping me."

"It's my absolute pleasure."

This respite was short, but it was a beautiful ten minutes. It was long enough to take a few deep breaths. The little ones crawled back over and the four of us snuggled into three seats while Zac took a well-deserved breather.

"I hope you are enjoying your moment," I whispered as I removed a baby foot from my chin. To say it would be a long four hours would be an understatement.

There might have been a competition for who was having the worst flight.

Contestant A: The bald man in front of Zac who had a sticker affixed to the back of his head. Zac couldn't catch Austin in time and had to profusely apologize.

Contestant B: The young man next to Zac who at one point was surrounded by a baby on his left pulling his ear and a stranger to his right puking into the complimentary bags.

Contestant C: Me, despite buying five seats, having three children sit on top of my lap, and a husband stuck a row in front of me (we weren't about to disturb the nauseated man's nap).

By the time the plane landed at 11:45 p.m., we were all, let's say, done.

It took about fifteen minutes to deplane. While waiting, I decided I should try to rectify some of the carnage we had left behind. It didn't feel right to have someone spend their New Year's Eve removing Dora's plastic head from between the seats. I turned to the flight attendant and asked for a garbage bag. She ignored my request and headed toward the back to gather her own belongings and reapply her lipstick. *She must have some big New Year's plans*, I thought. I motioned for my husband to gather our troops, who, now having access to a completely empty plane, were playing a fun game of hide-and-seek in the aisles.

My ladybug warrior smiled at me as she left the plane. "Have a wonderful holiday," she called.

"Thank you! Laila is a lucky little girl." I smiled in her direction.

The flight attendant, wearing her coat and holding her bags, appeared in the aisle.

I tried to explain, "Sorry, we are moving. Just trying to clean up a little bit."

"Oh my god, get off the plane already."

Oh no. Nope. I was one minute away from a complete Mom freak-out. I literally had lollipop sticks in my hair and my full bladder suggested my earlier bathroom schedule plan had been ineffective.

"Did you perhaps not see us on this flight? We were the family in row twenty-five. We are the parents who can barely keep their children controlled in a living room but attempted to do so in a twenty-inch space because they deserve to see their Grammy and Gramps for the holidays. We have one child who is so terrified to be on a plane that we had to practice it for months. And we have infant twins. Twins. We received more help from strangers on this flight than from you. And now, when we ask for an extra thirty seconds to try to pick up some of the excess garbage, we are clearly bothering you by holding up your New Year's Eve plans."

Except I didn't say any of this. My instincts told me it wasn't worth the battle. I venomously muttered behind clenched teeth, "We are clearly trying."

I don't know what prevented me from my tirade. I thought about turning around. I thought about writing a letter, but I never did that either. I tried not to think about that flight attendant. I preferred to focus on Laila, a sweet little girl somewhere whose loving grandmother happily held the children of a stranger, even if they did stick their fingers in her diet cola.

CHAPTER 53
Next Stop—Home

Every night, we attempt a bedtime book. It is more successful when we divide and conquer, but if we want all three of them to focus, we will pull out *We're All Wonders*, by R. J. Palacio, the children's version of her novel, *Wonder*.

The first time we read the book, I sat my three children on the floor and said, "This is our new book about kindness." I watched their faces absorb the illustrations of a boy with only one eye, a boy learning to navigate the world and asking other people to change the "way they see."

"Where is his eye, Mommy?" Jordan asked.

"He only has one," I responded.

"Isn't he sad? How does he see?" Oliver's and Austin's questions overlapped each other.

"Let's read the story to find how," I stated.

"I like his dog," Austin said as he tried to pet the pages.

It was the first time we read a hardcover book without destroying the pages. It was the first time we sat for more than one minute as we read a story together. Maybe they liked the illustrations. Maybe they could sense my excitement. Maybe they were learning.

This was an important observation for me. It allowed me to merge my professional world with my personal one. My studies as an educator have concentrated in one area: storytelling. What stories are told? Who gets to tell them? How does power influence storytelling?

My teaching philosophy is rooted in Rudine Sims Bishop's theory of window and mirror texts, which states that individuals need to see themselves reflected in literature.[2] The lack of finding yourself depicted sends a message that you are devalued in society.

I remember searching bookstores to find pictures of children in orthotics or using sign language. I wanted Jordan to see herself in the pages she was reading. With each bookseller or librarian, I was handed books about kindness or animals. They were wonderful books, but the images were not concrete enough for her to understand the parallels. I knew the books that depicted kids with disabilities were being written, they just weren't a part of the mainstream. I had to search harder to find them.

Here's why that is so problematic. Let's say a school district has several elementary schools, and their inclusion model has an opportunity for children with the highest needs to be in a program together. This program will either be located in one building, or rotate throughout the different elementary schools. Which means, it is possible that a neurotypical child may not meet a peer with a disability until middle school. When you add this to the work of David T. Mitchell and Sharon L. Snyder from their research *Narrative Prosthesis: Disability and the Dependencies of Discourse*, which states most people adopt attitudes about disability from books and film more than personal interactions, it becomes especially important what messages those books are sending.[3]

This is at the heart of the argument about why we not only need "mirror texts," but also "window texts" to convey accurate depictions

2. Rudine Sims Bishop, "Mirrors, Windows, and Sliding Glass Doors," *Perspectives: Choosing and Using Books for the Classroom* 6, no. 3 (Summer 1990).

3. David T. Mitchell and Sharon L. Snyder, Narrative Prosthesis: Disability and the Dependencies of Discourse (Ann Arbor, MI: University of Michigan Press, 2000).

about disabilities. Too often, protagonists with disabilities are either written to exist as a source of inspiration or pity. What would it take for a character with a disability to be in the story *with* their disability and not because of it?

There are children with special needs in every neighborhood. Real children who do not solely exist to be the life lesson at the end of the story. Without accurate storytelling, we do not have enough messaging to answer the natural curiosity of children. When we leave so much unsaid, we are only perpetuating stigmas.

When the days are hard enough just to figure out how to sneak another vegetable into their meal, it seems almost overwhelming to remember how to encourage our children to be both validated and empathetic. Here's the short answer: notice your stories. Find texts that incorporate the beautiful intersectionality of real life. Find the stories that depict people of different abilities, races, genders, socioeconomic statuses. Include the stories that interrupt the stigmas. Then fill your bookshelves, your social media influences. It's work that starts right at home.

We read "Mommy's favorite story" several times a week. Each time, the kids ask different questions and I continue my mission to model empathy and kindness. As it turned out, they didn't need much of a push. A few weeks into the book, the boys were drawing. Oliver proudly held up his paper.

"Look, Mommy," he said, smiling.

"Kind boy!" Austin cheered.

"Mommy. I drew the kind boy. I love him."

I hung it on the wall. Jordan walked by and kissed it.

During another evening, Zac sat down with the kids for a story. Jordan grabbed a book and began to "read" from the pages. Jordan, now age seven, had learned some key sight words, which was a huge, unfolding victory. She was not able to read this book, and therefore was making up her own story (which sounded exactly like the plot of *Aladdin*). The boys had memorized the book and were very frustrated that she was not saying the correct words on the page.

"Daddy!" they screamed. "Jordan is talking about Jasmine and this book is about monsters. She is doing it wrong." Zac and I have yet to identify whether Jordan recognizes her own delays, but her bowed head and discarding the book on the floor gave us some indication that she knew she wasn't meeting her brothers' standards.

"Oliver and Austin," Zac began, "remember the kind boy. He showed us things were different and that was okay. Jordan can read the book how she wants to and then you can each take a turn." I love when Zac uses his teaching voice on the children; it is so effective.

After Jordan's turn, she was tired and ready for bed. As Zac tucked her in, I heard him compliment her on her beautiful storytelling. I rested with the boys and let them choose another story to read. Austin picked a Daniel Tiger story where a new character named Chrissy comes to play with them. He snuggled into bed and said, "This is my favorite story because Chrissy has my shoes." He opened the page and pointed to her leg braces, which looked exactly like the ones Austin had resting in the corner of the room.

"That's so cool!" Oliver cheered. "They are just like yours."

"Just like mine," Austin echoed. "Mama read."

With one small story at a time, we can help the world to love a little bigger.

CHAPTER 54
Love Notes Shouldn't Be Typed

Zac and I took a weekend away from the kids. The goal was to do nothing.

During this quiet time, I grabbed a book from my favorite bookstore. It was by a best-selling author known for beach reads. In this novel, a woman learns her child is not meeting her milestones and the woman might have to call Early Intervention services to help her daughter learn to walk. The protagonist thinks it is her fault and, through a long string of events, has an affair. At the conclusion of the novel, all is discovered, all is forgiven, and the last page ends with the baby taking a step. Happy ending. There is nothing wrong with your baby, leading lady, so you can go back to your husband now. There was an underlying message that this woman's actions were justified because the paperwork to get an evaluation was just too stressful for her. More problematic platitudes.

That summer read had the opposite impact of its intended effect. I thought it was going to be about a sweet British lady who falls in love with the neighborhood maintenance man, not about perpetuating stereotypes of ableism in our country. This book has sold thousands of copies on the premise that being unfaithful is okay because you might have a child with special needs.

I was angry.

I was spending my precious time with my husband, fixating on fictionalized conflicts. I was concerned about the message being sent for parents, real people trying to make it through the day. Parents are not superheroes. Special needs parents do not have magical potions. We are all just people doing the best we can.

I am not certain if I was more upset that the book was perpetuating the stigmas I was fighting against or because I also wanted a time-out from parenting. I was desperate for an escape. Here I was, having a weekend with my wonderful husband, and I was too tired to enjoy his company.

I thought of all the things I wanted to say to Zac. *I am worried my stress adds to your stress. I feel guilty that I want time alone, and when I get it, I feel too guilty to enjoy it. I am nostalgic for our days before children. I am regretful I don't have the energy to put into our marriage the way I hoped I would. I am sorry our love notes have dwindled to a Post-it sticky note that says, "I gave her medicine." I feel like we are living in a world of "no" when we used to dream about the possibility of "yes." I'm worried our children don't get enough attention and the chaos isn't healthy for them.* But of course, I was too tired to say any of this.

"Zachary? I didn't like my book."

"Want to go to the bookstore to get another one?"

"Yes." *Yes, I do.*

When we came home from our weekend, there was a drawing waiting for us. I love children's artwork. I have fond memories of diligently sketching and walking up to my preschool teacher, who was trained to say, "Leah. It's beautiful. Tell me what you see." I would clearly point out the picture of my family and she would write in black Sharpie marker: *Leah and her father.* Then, when I handed the picture to my dad, he could say, "Why, Leah, what a lovely picture of you and the family," thus reinforcing my talent. In full disclosure, my drawing skills have not progressed since age five; everyone still lacks a neck and wears a belt.

This time it was one of Oliver's quiet-time drawings. His preschool teacher recognized he needed a space to be without anyone knocking over his tower or coloring on his paper. *Don't we all, kiddo. Why do you think Mommy and Daddy just left for the weekend?* He handed us a giant paper, full of colors and intersecting lines. The teacher's black marker read: *This is a picture of my house. Inside my house is a rainbow.*

What I call chaos, he calls home.

"Mommy. Did you see what I wrote?"

"Yes, honey. It's the best thing I have read in a long time."

CHAPTER 55
Birds, Bees, and Chromosomes

When I was around six, my father told me where babies came from. We were riding on the back of a sit-down lawn mower. I'm not sure I caught all the details.

After the birth of each of my children, I decided it was a great time to tell them the stories of the birds and the bees. I held each of my newborn children and jokingly said to my husband, "Well, that parenting task is done. What's next? The electoral process?"

When they were a bit older, we wanted the boys to learn what cri du chat was. It was a mature conversation, and we knew it would be a long time before they understood the complexity of Jordan's diagnosis, but perhaps giving them some language at an early age would demystify some of the societal stigmas we fight against. I wanted to underscore the facts that she is not a burden, she does not need pity, and she is simply their big sister.

This conversation has naturally evolved as they have gotten older. Around age two, Austin discovered all the pages of his favorite book were missing. "Uh-oh. Jordie broke this too."

Seemed like a good enough time to try.

"Boys." I gathered them onto my lap. "Sometimes your sister doesn't do good listening because she has a rare genetic syndrome called cri du chat. That means she may need more help to do things."

"Okay."

"So sometimes she needs a little more time."

"Okay."

"Sometimes she may do things differently than you do."

"Okay."

"Also, tomorrow a dinosaur is coming to your school."

"Okay."

Of course I knew they were too little, but it felt good to say it aloud.

They might not have understood why she destroyed their things, but as they got older, they knew enough to protect them. When Jordan decided she wanted whatever toy they were playing with, Oliver would move to the other side of the room, waving anything random, and say, "Jordie, I have a present for you." When she ran over to where he was, he quickly closed the gate behind her. He did it gently, but the message was received. Not to Jordan—she was never deterred—but to us as parents.

These boys were craving a bit of alone time. They needed space that was just for them. Oliver would ask for it by stating, "I need a minute alone to talk to myself," and then curl up in his bedroom. Austin was far more instinctual—he would just hit if she got too close.

These interactions were probably like how other siblings were behaving, but I was sensitive to it. I already felt guilty that the boys didn't get the attention she did—child number two and three rarely do—but they were also twins, and she required far more than older siblings usually need. I wanted to make sure they weren't receiving unintended messages about where our priorities as parents were.

When we found the drawing of five faces with one crossed out, we called Austin and Oliver into the room. Jordan was in her bedroom, playing with her dolls. The boys stood with their heads down, shoulder to shoulder, knowing we were about to have a chat.

"It's our family," Austin said.

"Why is this person crossed out?" Zac asked.

No one spoke.

We used our parenting voices. "Boys. What is this?"

Oliver stammered, "When you ... uh ... can't run, they cross off ... uh ... the sign. Or if you ... uh ... can't talk on the phone, there is a line."

This explanation did not solve anything. Now we used our teaching voices. "Please explain."

Oliver motioned his hand with a circle and a line through it. "You know, you cross it out. When you can't do something. The kissing. We crossed it out."

"Oh? Is this a picture of Jordan? Is she kissing and you crossed it off?"

"Yes," Austin said sheepishly. "She kisses too much. We wanted to tell her no more kissing."

Every night, Jordan would chase them with the hope of kissing their faces. If she was successful, she would pull their necks into her body and plant juicy kisses on them. They hated this. Her kisses were reminiscent of eighth-grade spin the bottle, lots of passion and too much teeth.

It initially looked like my sons were trying to extradite their sister, which was enough to break my heart, but they were simply frustrated. Zac helped the boys tell Jordan for the fortieth time that they did not like when she kissed them so much. Jordan, undeterred, kissed them and ran off to her room, gleefully shouting, "Night, brothers!"

As I tucked Oliver in, he said in a soft voice, "Mama?"

"Yes, sweetie."

"How can we get the cri du chat to go away?"

I knew this question would come eventually, and I knew it would come repeatedly.

"Honey, it's not going to—"

"Can't we just find it? The number five?"

Oliver had recently been exploring his new book and learning about chromosomes. It was incredible watching his understanding develop.

"No, honey. It is part of who Jordan is and we love her for it. It just takes her a little longer to learn how to do things, so we help her when we can."

"Okay," he said quickly. Then he added, "Next time you get a child, can you get one who doesn't kiss so much?"

"Sure, but there won't be any more children."

"I'm sure we can find one at Target, Mama. And a new tractor car."

Maybe in a few years, when we cover the birds and the bees again, we will review chromosomes too.

CHAPTER 56
Crayon Wings

A child's breakdown is one of the prerequisite badges of parenthood, and no matter how many times they pry their little fingers under the door of the bathroom to get your attention, throw food at you from their car seat, or smash the crayon because it is "too red," you know it has to stop eventually.

When Jordan experienced one of these epic meltdowns in public, we just scooped her up and carried her out of the situation. That was how we handled the dish-breaking moment at the Odyssey Diner, the thrashing in the turtle pond at the Norwalk Aquarium, and the destruction of the gift shop at the Bronx Zoo. As her parents, we learned the signs of an impending episode like an unspoken dance. Forget the infamous swing move we used to bust out at weddings; the intricate "I'll basket-carry her away" was far more impressive. Especially as our darling girl grew heavier every year.

It took some time to adjust to the staring from other children or the purposeful avoidance of other parents. The *get your kid under control* glare, or the *your child is far too old to behave like this* scowl both have a way of burning themselves into your parenting self-esteem file. Each time Jordan melted down in public, I tried to ignore the creeping guilt that told me the trip was too much and we should have just stayed home where she was comfortable. I pushed down the jealousy I felt toward other parents strolling through the neighborhood, or swallowed the resentment I carried while watching other mothers and daughters together. I learned to ignore them. I had to. When Jordan had a meltdown, the goal was simple: make her safe and calm. Parental shaming had no place in the equation.

When she tantrums, it's as if her body cannot absorb all the energy at once. She physically needs to get rid of it, whether that means hitting, biting, or thrashing on the floor. It takes a toll on the whole family, but on no one more than Jordan. It's as if her rational self has lifted from her body and she is nothing but raw emotion. When she is done, there's the script. She will whimper, "I sorry. I never do it again," but of course we know there will be an "again."

When it is over, there is this moment of regrouping. As her parent, it takes a moment to recover. We have revved ourselves up so much to protect her that we don't have enough time to decompress before the next event happens. Therefore, we never release the stress and it comes up when we don't realize it (usually when these beautiful humans refuse to go to bed). Yet all this time, Austin and Oliver are watching. Always watching.

When the boys had enough language to begin to ask what was going on with Jordan, we would try to explain that she needed a bit more time. When I need an extra moment, I always say, "Mommy is also a person. Please give her a minute."

They think this is hysterical, as if Mommy momentarily thought she was a dinosaur or a race car or something. Zac and I can't be sure if we are modeling the best behavior for them, but like all things, we try. As it turns out, all that watching has helped them to become "ladybug warriors" in their own way.

During an especially challenging outing to the Westchester mall, Jordan was done. Her legs were too lethargic to leave, her tongue was too tired to talk, so all she could do was flail and wail. Austin and Oliver—correction, Superman Austin and Superman Oliver— were watching this unfold. They had been rummaging through an

assortment of miscellaneous Mommy items from my coat pocket—
Matchbox cars, a windup toy, two lollypop sticks, and one bobby
pin—before choosing their prize: broken crayons. Jordan's crying got
their attention.

With their little capes flying behind them, they swooped in: "We
will help you, Jordie!"

"Boys, Jordan needs a minute. Go to the car with Mommy."

But they pushed past Zac.

"Jordie. You don't have a cape. You need wings." Their little voices
blended as they circled around her. "These will help you," they cheered.

Zac and I stood back to watch the superheroes take their crayons to
simultaneously draw wings all over Jordan's body, on the sleeves of her
jacket, on each of her shoes, and one final one on her back.

"Okay. Now you can fly." They giggled in unison as only
twins could.

She stood up and walked directly into the elevator.

Oliver placed the crayon in my pocket and the boys confidently
marched behind her.

"Mommy, hold these for Jordie—for next time."

CHAPTER 57
For Sale:
One Screaming Child

Jordan was in a passionate relationship with Target. As her language developed, so did her ability to work Target into most sentences.

Example A: "Leah, I am going to make hamburgers tonight for dinner," Zac called from the kitchen.

Jordan materialized. "I have an idea. We could go to Target and get cookies."

Example B: "Jordan, I have to work late tonight, so Barbara is going to stay with you."

"Here's the deal, Mommy: I will take her to Target so she isn't lonely."

The issue with going to Target was that Jordan couldn't just browse. She needed to purchase something. It came to the point where we wouldn't take her to Target unless there was a specific gift she'd earned. Otherwise, it was just a bit unfair to all of us to force her into a situation knowing that it wouldn't have her desired outcome. I knew we would reach a time when we could do this without the epic meltdown, but we weren't there yet and we couldn't handle one more tiny plastic doll with excessive hair.

However, sometimes Jordan achieved an incredible milestone, and then all her wishes would come true. This was the case when she no longer needed diapers in any capacity. We had been working on it for seven years. We were so proud of her, I would have bought her the entire electronics department. It would be cheaper than the diapers.

We skipped toward the bull's-eye logo. She had her sparkly purse filled with twelve dollars for one Hairdorables, another plastic invention with oversized features and colorful hair that she would inevitably disrobe and then lose. She pulled me to the aisle: empty shelf.

"Hmm. Looks as if they are sold out. What if you got a Pikmi Pop instead, Jordan?"

"No." She planted herself on the floor.

Here we go.

I sat with her. We talked out a plan for about five minutes. This tactic was not working.

I redirected. There were other wonderful things in Target that she could take home.

"No."

I changed the conversation. Perhaps ice cream would be more fun, or even a manicure.

"No."

She looked so beautifully sad. Her curly hair was escaping from beneath her blue wig, and she had placed both hands under her chin, squishing her cheeks into her furrowed brow. I was tired. All the toys ended up at the bottom of a donation bag eventually—did it really matter which one we bought?

I called Zac to let him know we would be delayed. I considered asking for someone to bring us some sleeping bags, as Jordan looked like she was making herself comfortable.

"Okay, Jordan. I know you're disappointed, but I think if we stay here too long, someone is going to think you are for sale."

She liked that. It was a new line to the script. A woman appeared in the aisle. She had clearly been listening while browsing the toys, perhaps for her grandchildren. She smiled at me with such warmth that, under this fluorescent lighting, I could swear she was Glinda the Good Witch.

"Hello. I am looking to buy a little girl who is wearing a blue wig, and here you are. I was wondering how much you cost."

Jordan giggled again.

"Oh, well, this particular model is very expensive." I patted Jordan's head. "She comes with a variety of wigs, not just blue, so you have to consider the total cost."

Jordan loved this game.

"Well, I would love to buy you for my grandson. I heard your mommy say you were for sale."

"I'm not for sale." Jordan chuckled. "That's silly."

"Well, I guess you should go with your mommy then before someone thinks you are one of the toys."

Jordan soaked in the attention. I was only a little concerned she was going to generalize this "I'm for sale" activity as the new way to interact in stores.

I had learned the hard way about Jordan's overgeneralization tendencies. The routine is what brings her comfort, but we aren't always sure what will stick. We learned this during one Halloween when Jordan was two. At the time, she was fearful of Halloween, but we thought it would be an enjoyable skill to work on for her (who doesn't want candy?). We practiced by going to her therapist's house, so she would see the individual steps. She would carry her pumpkin basket, ring the doorbell, sign hello, and then receive a piece of candy. We practiced several times until Jordan felt comfortable. After we were finished, we sat on the couch and looked at her therapist's goldfish while the adults chatted briefly.

The evening of Halloween, a plainly dressed Jordan (because, ironically, on Halloween she was not interested in wearing a costume) had carried her pumpkin bucket, rung the first doorbell, signed hello, and received a piece of candy. Then she pushed past the elderly woman and sat on her couch. They shared a meatball before we went home. That was the only house we visited that year. We were hoping enough time would pass before the following Halloween, or we would have to explain to our neighbors why Jordan was insisting on sitting in their living rooms with them.

Although there was now a chance that every time we went to a store, Jordan would not leave until a stranger tried to buy her, it was a risk I was willing to take to make some headway toward the exit. Sitting on the floor in Target, Jordan egged on her new friend. "I cost a lot."

"She costs a lot," I repeated, just in case the woman couldn't understand the banter.

The woman smiled.

Jordan stood up and said, "That's silly. You cannot buy me." She cackled so loudly, she revealed her tiny dimple, and I was worried she was laughing so hard that she was going to have an accident.

I took advantage of the momentum to get her moving toward the exit sign. There was no time to express my gratitude to the woman. However, as we turned the corner, I saw her watching us, as if to say, *I'm still here if needed.* I sent her all my gratitude via a fleeting wave and then ordered the Hairdorables on my Amazon app as soon as Jordan was snapped into her car seat.

Not a lot of people feel comfortable joining another family's interaction. It's the unwritten rule that you mind your own business. I am often asked what I would want people to do or say if they observe a scenario like the one I just described. My response is that it is not a special needs issue; it is universal. If we see a situation with someone seemingly in need, we simply extend a "Do you need anything?" It won't be offensive, inappropriate, or out of line. It is kindness—simple and effective.

CHAPTER 58

Everyone Made It
Through the Day Alive

I have reduced my standards so that a successful day is measured by the fact that I have kept everyone alive. It's a bonus day if I can also cut three sets of fingernails. Three children meant we were completely outnumbered. We needed to rely on a zone defense as our parenting style, and it wasn't always effective. Before the twins were born, when Jordan merely whimpered, time would freeze and I would run across mountains to soothe her. Now, one kid rode down the stairs in a laundry basket, another fell backward off the couch, and the third smacked into the corner of the table. It was a quick inventory of who needed us first. It is quite the day when someone who has fallen on his or her head doesn't become the priority.

When I really stopped to think about how many opportunities there were for my children to get hurt, it was paralyzing. Austin, while walking, was still a delicious wobbler. Jordan had difficulty navigating the stairs, and Oliver believed he could fly.

I tried to arrange for backup whenever possible so I did not have to be alone when my body contracted in fear. I preferred to share this relaxing experience with a loved one.

This time it was Grammy. We were visiting the library on our holiday vacation while Zac and his dad were off getting some bonding time. Oliver, must have needed a bit of space, because as soon as we hit the children's section, he started running laps. I remained fairly cool. I left the other kids with my stepmother-in-law and patiently trotted after him. "Come back, honey."

Lap two was more of the paranoid phase: *Did he run into the elevator?*

Lap three: *Man, I must restart my yoga class. I'm getting a little sore.*

Lap four: *We are so getting kicked out.*

It seemed as if Oliver's speed had picked up, and I couldn't determine if I was chasing him or if he was now chasing me. There was no enjoyment in this game. I did not know where he was, and he was not responding to his name.

There it was. The *boom* of what could only be one thing: a head into a blunt object. Instant wailing.

I turned the corner and found a young mother holding him. "He ran into the corner of the chair. I think his nose is bleeding."

He uncurled himself from this kind stranger and exposed a crime scene's worth of blood. "Okay, just a nosebleed. Those stop quickly," she said.

"Yes, thank you."

I scooped him into my arms, profusely thanked her, and prepared myself. She was right. A typical nosebleed doesn't take that long to stop, except this is the child with ITP. I prepared for three facts: this nosebleed would last awhile, we were about to have a lot of blood, and we would likely require a bit of assistance.

Austin and Jordan took their positions. They have learned what to do when this happens. Austin determined early on that his job was to find two lollipops, one for him and one for Oliver. He reached right into my backpack and then shoved the lollipop in Oliver's blood-soaked face. Jordan always searched for the towel. She independently went to the library restroom and came back with one solitary tissue. *Thanks, sweetie.*

The librarian, who had clearly noticed us since our arrival (I mean, how could you miss us?), called behind her. "You can have more than one. It looks like you might need it."

"Okay." Jordan went back and got two.

My children's support of one another was almost enough to comfort the Jackson Pollock blood painting we were creating. Grammy and I went into action. She secured the wipes and we began to rid the scene of blood: the floor, the chair, my clothes, his face, the lollipop.

As we all huddled together, Oliver whimpered, "Do I need to go to the hospital?" The rules were that only spontaneous nosebleeds signified low platelets; this was just the wrong head in the wrong place at the wrong time. The librarian approached us with the entire box of tissues. "Do you need anything? Will he be okay?"

I bashfully assured her we just needed a bit of time and we would be leaving shortly. Everyone stayed exceptionally calm. Thank goodness Grammy always knew what to do in an emergency and I didn't have to manage this stress alone.

When the bleeding subsided, we dragged ourselves toward the exit. We lacked a bit of the luster we'd had when we'd first entered. Piles of red-stained backpacks, coats, and children really made a statement.

The librarian tenderly stopped us. "Excuse me, miss. I think you should take this box of tissues. It's just a box of tissues, but I really think you need it more than we do." She paused and added sheepishly, "I also hope your day gets a bit better. Enjoy your time with your children."

Her words were so gentle. Maybe it was the Southern accent, but I felt like if it had been acceptable to do so, she would have just scooped me up and held me. It was just a box of one-ply tissues, but it was a kind gesture. It wasn't pity; it was support. It was truly appreciated.

If you ever find yourself in the Frisco area, I recommend stopping by the second floor of the library. There you will find one of the kindest strangers I have ever met, and I am confident she will share her tissues with you, even if you don't leave a pool of blood near the fiction section.

CHAPTER 59
Game Time

When you anticipate having a child, it's only natural to think about what family traditions you will pass on to them. Holiday meals, vacation destinations, or, in my case, the ice cream cone during the second period of the New Jersey Devils hockey game. It had a hard chocolate coating, a decadent treat that was a welcome change from our home "junk-food" stash that only contained raisins. When I was a child, my parents, Rachel, and I found our happy place in Section 122—and I became very popular at recess after sharing my new vocabulary of curse words.

I received my Scott Niedermayer jersey as a bat mitzvah present in 1994 and wore it through both of my pregnancies. It contained the stains of twenty years of that ice cream and some now-faded and illegible autographs of hockey greats. I made sure Jordan had a matching one for the first time we took her to the stadium to continue this tradition.

Zac and I couldn't wait to include her. We created a social story, detailing the events of the day to allow her to anticipate the steps she would take to attend the game, obviously including the second-period ice cream break. We planned with her therapists and bought new soundproof headphones to ensure the stadium noise wouldn't hurt her sensitive ears. My dad, escorting us to the game, spent an hour in the car, showing her pictures of hockey players and watching clips of the game. When we arrived at the arena, she was impressed by the colorful lights outside.

We lasted five minutes.

It was all too much. The stadium was too loud, there were too many people, the sound was beyond deafening. She wailed and said, "No. I go home."

We returned to the car. With traffic, we pulled into the driveway just as the buzzer on the last period was sounding.

Zac and I felt defeated. It wasn't just about the hockey game. It was the recognition that even with all of our formal training and incredible milestones, there were experiences Jordan still could not tolerate, starting with anything in a larger space: movie theaters, plays, arenas.

My parents, always ready for a challenge, had a bit more energy for this task than I could take on. While I was managing the day-to-day sensory needs, they were continual optimists that we could help her to access this space.

"We will get there," they reassured me.

I didn't believe them.

A year later, my father called to suggest we try it again. "Our record is to beat five minutes. It's worth a try."

"Jordan, would you like to go to a hockey game with us?" my parents enthusiastically invited her.

"No, thank you," she said calmly. "It's too loud. Take my brothers. I go to Target."

"Well, how about a movie?"

Like I said, always the optimists.

Zac and I created a new social story, a map with pictures of the events of the day, to allow her to anticipate the steps she would take to attend the movie, clearly including the snacks she would eat in her seat. I felt very doubtful. My dad, ready to be her date for the day, attempted to put on her shoes.

"No. I don't want to go to movie. Too loud. I only want to go to Target." She was beyond defiant. When Jordan started to perseverate about a topic, she talked in circles, as if she were reciting a script inside her brain. It could last for hours if no one interrupted her thought process.

Meanwhile, Austin and Oliver were standing by the door in their tiny Devils tees, anticipating their first hockey game. The plan was to have Jordan attend a movie with my parents while the rest of us would have a family date to see the Devils. The image of my boys' small hands inside their large, red, foam fingers, patiently waiting for our attention, broke me. They deserved the same excitement and buildup to continue this family tradition, and now there was a chance they might not get to go at all. The situation escalated and we were almost at the point where Jordan would shut down for the entire day—meaning no one was going anywhere.

I paused and regrouped. I returned to the facts.

Step 1: What did I observe? She screamed at the thought of the movie. She perseverated on going to Target.

Step 2: What did I know? She had no mental map for what a movie theater looked like. Even though we have prepared her for it, she wasn't able to access in her brain where she might possibly be going. Target was safe. Target was fun. I had to remove Target as an option.

Step 3: The plan. Zac and I divided and conquered—as we do best. He corralled the boys into the car while ideas stumbled out of my mouth.

"Jordan, remember when you had to go to the bathroom last year and we stopped at the funny mall and ran so fast?"

She stopped hitting me and looked up. "Yes." She smiled.

"Yes! That is where the movie theater is." Halfway there. "I have to call Target now to see if they are open today. I think they might be cleaning it."

Thanks, seventh-grade play for the inspiration for the fake phone call.

"Hello, Target. I was wondering if you were open today. Oh, you aren't? [Insert dramatic disappointed face.] That is too bad. Would you be open later today? My daughter was really hoping to come with her grandparents. Oh? Really? [Raise eyebrows.] I didn't realize you needed to close the store to clean the floors. Yes, that is important. Well, what do you suggest she do instead? Oh, I also heard *Mary Poppins Returns* was a great movie. Well, yes. You have a great day too."

I hung up the phone.

"Mommy, Target closed?"

"Yes, honey."

"Okay. Bye, Mommy. I go to the movies with Grandma and Grandpa!" she cheered. She literally pushed me out the door. "Get out of here."

The rest of the story is a retelling from my courageous parents. I was off having an adventure with my husband and sons. It was my privilege to have a moment to be present with them.

Not only did Jordan watch *Mary Poppins Returns*, but she did so in a theater without any sensory modifications. She voted on each preview, Coliseum style, with a thumbs-up or thumbs-down. When the movie came on, she just—sat. She snuggled into her large movie theater chair, mesmerized by the screen, consuming an entire bag of gummy bears and a sleeve of Oreo cookies. In seven years of her life, she had never sat so still for so long. When the final credits rolled, the lights came up upon a beautiful family image: an Oreo-caked grandchild, a proud grandfather, and a tearful grandmother. They described it as one of the best days they had ever had with her.

"I want to see it again," she told me when she got home and every day for the next four months.

That evening we gathered back together to share the day's events. It was more than a movie and a hockey game; it was another cross-out on the list of the things they said she wouldn't do. It gave me perspective for the future. There may be activities she would never experience, but we could continue to stretch her world one event at a time. She deserved some leisure breaks with her grandparents, and my sons deserved a chance to learn why the second-period ice cream cone was truly legendary.

CHAPTER 60
Moore Mayhem

It was quite surprising how long we went before someone needed stitches. I mean, really, we were just one missed step away from an emergency room run.

I went first. When you open a car door into your head, it means a few things. You are probably moving too fast and should remove your head before making contact with the metal siding, and there are better ways to get a sick day from work. Three stitches and one tube of Mederma scar cream later, I was back in action.

I was grateful to be first. When my children get hurt, it feels like my uterus contracts, as if my body is trying to absorb their pain for them.

Oliver was next. He always beats to his own drum, so rather than getting stitches, the doctor glued his eyelid back together after a nasty run-in with the couch.

"That's silly. You only put glue on paper," Oliver said. But he thought the eye cover he had to wear was very cool.

Austin upped the stakes a bit. When he tripped over his bike and fell headfirst into concrete, the open wound on his forehead suggested it was more than the bandage drawer could handle. I shoved all three kids in the car, asked Oliver to hold a towel to his brother's gushing forehead, and rushed to the doctor. In my panic, I did not bring shoes for Jordan, snacks, or a cell phone. I did bring three screaming children into the waiting room.

This situation invited pandemonium for the already chaotic Moore family. Austin, who struggles with his own sensory needs, was not a fan of being held down while a doctor put a needle into his head. They needed to strap him to a board to keep his body still, which only made the screaming worse. This wouldn't have been so challenging except shoeless Jordan thought it would be a fun game to turn off the lights on the doctor. I tried to extend my Inspector Gadget arms to reach both a wailing Austin and a naughty Jordan, but ultimately I had to divide and conquer. I bribed a now crying Oliver to sit by Austin's side so I could restrain Jordan from the light switch. The nurse practitioner looked at each of my children and said snidely, "You know, it is not helpful when she turns off the lights."

No shit, lady.

Our exodus was dramatic. Before piling back into the car, we collapsed into the CVS next door. "Get any candy you want." It was the mom equivalent to, "Next round's on me!"

The checkout girl smiled at my haggard family. "He needed stitches next door," I mumbled.

"Oh." She pulled back her sleeve, revealing a long scar across her arm. "Look, when I was a little girl, I got stitches too. You know what made it better?" She winked at Austin. "M&M's." Then she handed him his treat. She looked up at me. "Do you need any cream for the car?"

I handed her my money, gathered the kids, and smiled. "Thanks, but we already have it!"

We made it almost a full year without any trauma. Everyone's scars were healing; they added character to our faces. Then Jordan started losing her teeth. In fact, the tooth fairy made three visits in one week. We didn't realize, but this meant Jordan had stopped chewing her food.

There is always an underlying pulse of fear for me when Jordan is eating. The memory of her choking as a newborn in the hospital had never left me. When I heard the sounds coming from the other side of the room, it took a minute to register what was happening. Her shoulders fell forward and her head was low.

"Jordan, you okay?"

No response.

"Jordan?" I raised my voice. She turned toward me. Where her voice should be, I heard only gasping.

I pulled her close to me and thrust my arms into her abdomen. I shouted for Zac and by the second attempt he was standing there. He took her from me, repeated the motion with more force, and expelled an orange slice from her throat.

She burst into tears. It was a glorious sound. You need air to wail.

We held her until she was herself again. She returned to coloring and I fanatically began cutting all her food into minuscule bites. While she regained her breath, Zac and I tried to do the same ...

... I hope one day I actually can.

CHAPTER 61
We Love a Routine

Every day we wait outside for a package we never ordered. It started as a gentle lie that became a helpful distraction.

It is inevitable that the moment Zac and I step out of the family room, we will hear the familiar screeching of, "Help! Stop it!"

I know at the bottom of the steps, Jordan will be launching for her brothers' necks so she can catch them in a passionate embrace. It would be enough to tousle their hair or give them a high five, but she loves a bit too fiercely and inadvertently hurts them. She is Elmyra Duff from my childhood show, *Tiny Toon Adventures*, clutching her brothers so ferociously that their cartoon eyes would pop. "I'm going to hug you and kiss you and love you forever." It's endearing, but no one wants to be on the receiving end of her loving attacks.

The boys rely on their new strategy. "Jordan, I have a surprise for you. It is upstairs if you want to see it." And then, like a small puppy, she follows them, where they once again separate her into a different room. She thinks it is part of the game.

"Jordan, why don't we do something else? Let's go see if a package arrived." My words are enough to unlock her focus. It gives everyone a bit of a break until her next urge.

We turn the squeaky knob of our 1930s front door, careful not to crack the glass window—again. She jumps outside to embrace the day. It doesn't matter if she is presented with the cascading sun, pounding rain, or unseasonably worrisome snow, Jordan walks with purpose onto the porch. Cars stopped at the stop sign in front of our house have the opportunity to observe Ms. Jordan in her full glory: her new favorite outfit. Adult-sized fuzzy gray slippers from what could be the Davy Crockett collection, fluorescent-yellow Minion pajamas positioned perfectly to reveal a sizeable butt crack, and atop her spiral curls is the Doc McStuffins hat she has been wearing vehemently since age two. This girl loves a routine. Sadly, trying to propose to her brothers has become one of them.

"Is it here, Mama?"

This is when I feel guilty about my ruse. She stands in front of me, crossing fingers on both her hands, staring up into the sky. I know there is no package, but still we wait.

It gets pretty dicey when mail actually arrives. She's decided that her beloved gift will not come in an envelope, so she isn't fazed by bills or pamphlets. The smile from the Amazon box or the anticipatory bull's-eye is what she longs for. She has stood defeated over toothpaste and toilet paper, but remains hopeful every hour, sometimes every ten minutes, that next time there will be something more.

So, every day we look. We wait outside for a package we never ordered.

I use it to get her physical therapy in. When Jordan is left to her own devices, she proves that her body is in need of input. That is the only explanation for the twelve eggs she cracked onto the carpet while I was in the bathroom.

"I'm making a small pool for my cake," she proceeded to explain before ice-skating in it.

For the sake of my carpet, I needed to find another way to expel her energy. The possibility of a package is enough to take the long journey, twenty-five steps, to the mailbox and provides an opportunity for tactile support. "Is it here, Mama?"

She grabs my hand, pulls her pajama pants down to reveal just a bit more tush, repositions her hat, and is ready to go. Together we push through the side gate, listening to the metal clasp crack on the splintering wood. We start the big climb, over a handful of pebbles strewn on the driveway, traverse across the front yard, and take the final leap off the rock wall to reach our destination. Crossed double fingers, hopeful eyes to the sky—alas, no package.

"Jordan, did your package come today?" my husband asks her every night at dinner. Most days she just giggles, but today she is eager to talk.

"No. It will come tomorrow. It's a Shopkins Choco Waffle," she finally informs us. "I ordered one."

While she has learned to open the washing machine to clean her Minions on the third day of every week, she has not yet independently ordered anything from Amazon. Leave that to her brothers, who have a running tab of $14.24.

This announcement is important. Now that we know what she thinks she is waiting for, we could at least attempt to find it.

"Well, let's check on it, Jordan. It hasn't arrived yet." Zac artfully keeps up the façade as Jordan is convinced her cherished item is on the way. He scours the internet and finally locates the item on eBay, one Squish-Dee-Lish Shopkins Choco Waffle. "Should be here in a few days," he says as he enters our PayPal information.

Seven watchings later of the *Minions*, thirty-five journeys to the mailbox, and far too many squeals of, "Help! Stop it!," reveal a brown package addressed just to her.

"My package is here!"

Practically tripping over her sagging pajama pants and oversized woolly slippers, Jordan takes her prize and throws it at her dad. The mandatory twenty-second hand-washing after touching the brown paper was not enough to slow her down. As she takes a deep breath, Zac pulls out the beloved item: a Shopkins Choco Waffle.

He places it gently into the palm of her hand.

She squints. "What happened?"

We gather as a family to look. It does not appear to be a toy. A key chain, perhaps. A dessert for Ant-Man. It is no larger than her thumbnail.

"It's so tiny!" Her laugh fills the kitchen.

There is something magical about her laugh. It radiates through her entire body and revitalizes any room.

"What happened to it?" she asks again and grabs her stomach, the sign of her heartiest laugh, almost enough to relieve her bladder.

When she has returned from the bathroom, and has completed another intense hand-washing, she pinches the item.

"Nah," she says as she tosses it into the crevices of the couch. "I'll wait for a new one." She walks to the front door.

Zac and I both know this tiny trinket is the only one on the internet, but of course we smile. "We'll go with you."

And we all go outside, fingers crossed, eyes to the sky, to see if a new package has indeed arrived.

CHAPTER 62
One Broadway,
Two Performances

"I am Avis!" Jordan cheered as she stepped off the bus. She threw her head back, shaking out her spiral curls. "THE MAGIC CARPET," she boasted, and flew into the house.

I texted everyone I knew. This was momentous—Jordan was going to be in her first play, Disney's *Aladdin Kids*. The theater environment had traditionally been too dark, the sound too loud, and the "hushed silence" of the crowd too preposterous. Zac and I had accepted that we might not be able to share something that felt so foundational to who we were as her parents with her in a traditional way. But truth be told, for our storytelling family, this was always a sore bruise. By seven, Jordan had gotten to an age where she was no longer scared, but rather overexcited. It was hard for her to remain quiet during a performance. Trying to be considerate of other patrons, we took her only to theaters where her enthusiastic outbursts would be appropriate. The children's production of *Cinderella* at a barn in my hometown in New Jersey seemed like a good place to start. Jordan was so engaged that when the prince, a four-foot-tall seventh-grade boy, was looking for the owner of the missing slipper, he walked off the stage, down the aisle, and asked Jordan if she wanted to try it on.

"No!" she shouted gleefully. There was that dimple again.

"Watching her enjoyment of this show made me enjoy it that much more," the generous couple behind us shared at the conclusion of the play.

We transferred this success to her own rehearsals. We had placed her script in a professional-looking folder and practiced her three lines with her nightly. She rehearsed every week after school for months. On the day of the performance, Jordan was stage-makeup ready long before the curtain call. Of course she was; she had woken up like that.

This was a huge day for Jordan. It was for us as her parents, too, but our experience of the night's events was vastly different from how Jordan perceived it.

Version 1: Jordan's Perspective

Whenever we drive past the high school where Jordan's play occurred, she points out the window, claps, and says, "That is where I had my big day." When we see anyone who was in the production, she runs up to them and reminds them what their part was for the play. We have never gotten her exact report of the night's events, but based on her reactions, it is safe to say it looked something like this.

The production begins with Jordan pushing through the stage curtain to meet the audience. She cannot be bothered to wait for the production to start. She enthusiastically waves to her adoring family, who are five rows back. They are clutching a bouquet of flowers to give to her after the show.

She is dressed in a fabulous, shoulder-length purple wig, with a three-foot curtain rod extending on either side of her shoulders to hold up her carpet costume. She looks incredible and like a walking liability. There are some giggles and the man next to me says, "How adorable."

"Oh, she's mine. Just wait."

Jordan is a star. She is animated, excited to be in front of an audience—she is everywhere. When it is time for Jordan's line, she speaks clearly and confidently, "Magic carpet at your service." Then she improvises some lines and adds, "Hop on for a ride—one, two, three, let's go!" and flies a first-grade Aladdin and Jasmine around the stage. She gets uproarious applause.

When the play ends, Jordan takes the bows she has practiced in her mirror. Except this time, it isn't just her reflection staring back: it is eighty-five friends and family members of her club. Austin and Oliver, standing up on their seats, cheer and wave. "Hi, Jordie. We see you in a play!"

Backstage, we find Jordan concluding her acceptance speech in the mirror. She spins mid-kiss to her reflection, flings her hair toward us, and says, "Did you see me, Daddy?" She pauses and points her chin to the sky. "I was incredible."

"Yes, you were, sweetie."

When we drive away from the school, she waves and whispers, "That was my big day." It is here she realizes the reflection in the mirror, the little girl dancing at Carnegie Hall, can come true. Maybe. For her, it is a beautiful night that she will dream about for days to come.

Version 2: Our Perspective

Someone once asked me what made Jordan happy. I responded without hesitation: Jordan.

She hears music in her head, so no matter where she is, she is a star. She gallops up and down the aisles of Costco. She walks into McDonald's and sings, "I'm back." Her life is a continual dance class for one, yet she is happy to welcome anyone to the party. She introduces herself to every stranger. There are some occasions where her bravado doesn't fit into societal norms. I don't take her to quiet temple services or events where she needs to display solemnity. We understand there is a time and place for her personality.

Then come the stares. When she was a small child, strangers absorbed her big personality as the sweet behavior of a child. Then she was politely ignored. The walker, the sign language, the braces made others not want to focus on us too much, as if to give us space to get through the situation. Now that Jordan is at the age where she should be completing math problems and reading independently, it seems as if people aren't sure what to do with this spirited, twirling child in a rainbow wig and a dance outfit.

Most days, the stares bounce right off me. I am the leader of her parade. This is a child who was told she would never [insert any number of things], and here she is making a scene in your store. *Good for her.* We used to struggle to get out of the house and now she wants to work at the cash register. *Wonderful.* The stares sting, however, when they come from within our community.

The evening of the play, I proudly walk her backstage. Jordan says "hello" to one of her castmates and tries to sit down.

"This seat is taken," the little girl replies, moving her backpack onto the seat.

Undeterred, Jordan sits alone. I, however, freeze. This is not a random student; this is someone Jordan has been in theater club with for over three months. Her coldness toward my child is piercing. I do not know what to do. When little girls in public stare at her, I often try to redirect the situation by telling them to come over and say hi. I wish I had said, "Please move your bag. My daughter will be sitting here," but I am ashamed to say I just absorbed the blow, secretly cursed her parents' child-rearing skills, and sat next to Jordan to reapply her makeup.

I touch base with her incredible aide and reinforce she will be close by to help Jordan. The plan is for her to remain on the stage, so if Jordan needs to be redirected, she can appear from the wings and help Jordan as needed. I remind her, "Sometimes she can get a bit overenthusiastic."

She smiles. "We are ready. We have practiced."

Jordan is indeed a star. She is animated, excited to be in front of an audience—she is everywhere. Including places where she shouldn't be. Before the play begins, Jordan bursts through the curtain to say hello to the audience. Zac and I wave at her to go back behind the velvet. We pass each other a knowing look.

When the production starts, Jordan bursts in front of the other children to speak into the microphone to tell them what is coming next in the play. She starts to perseverate about Mal's dad from Disney's *Descendants* and asks the audience who the president was when they were born. She repeats the same sentences several times before inviting everyone to her cousin's house for Thanksgiving. These are topics that are not related, not appropriate for the setting. The amplification of the microphone and the pacing of her language mean there are only four people who know what she is talking about: her bewildered parents and her little brothers. By this point, my cheeks turn red in humiliation.

I stand up to look for the aide. Where is she? Why is Jordan able to run around the stage without being gently redirected to her spot? I spot her in the audience holding the script, feeding kids their lines. Is there any adult on the stage to help Jordan refocus? When her curtain rod begins sawing into the neck of her classmates, why doesn't the director assist? I consider how I can get on the stage and help redirect her myself. After all, Zac and I are theater teachers. We teach nonverbal students on a daily basis how to engage in theater. We don't usually play the educator card, but there are few things we know how to do: teach theater, create appropriate modifications, and parent our child. Here we are faced with all three. This is why there is a plan to assure her success.

No one is following it.

The giggles start in the audience. The disapproving side glances from her fellow actors are too much for me to take; it doesn't matter that she isn't aware of them. When it is time for her line, she does a beautiful job. She says it proudly, clearly, and flies around the stage as the gorgeous carpet she is. However, I watch it with constricted breath. Is the applause and laughter after her line supportive, or is it at her expense? Is the audience looking at her with a piteous "good for her," or are they genuinely enjoying her performance? Are her cast members angry at their potential decapitation, or are they used to it from rehearsal?

The longer she is up there, running around the stage, the more opportunities there are for people to tease her. The more she interrupts the scene to talk, the more isolated she will become. When the play ends, Jordan extends the bows for a good two to three minutes by talking into the microphone. By this point, I am standing in the aisle and motioning for her to get off the stage.

I am a mess. Maybe it is just me. Maybe this is too close to home as a mother and theater teacher and it isn't as bad as I thought. After all, Jordan doesn't get embarrassed. But I do. What kind of mother am I to be embarrassed by my own child, especially when I have tirelessly fought for every morsel of her life? I am so uncomfortable with my discomfort.

I turn to Zac, my face burning hot.

"I am angry," he succinctly replies.

We turn to the boys, standing on the seats, proudly clapping for their big sister. We find her backstage, kissing her own reflection. Her classroom teacher greets us in the hallway. She has not seen the play, as she was working with another student backstage. "Well …" She greets us with a face full of sunshine. "How did it go?"

"We are so disappointed."

My emotions release and I cannot contain my tears. I turn to Jordan, who always notices when my eyes are wet. "Mommy is just so proud of you." And I am.

But I vent, "There was no support. She practically beheaded another child. She was left up there without anyone redirecting her. This is not what we practiced or prepared for. We have to leave. I will call you tomorrow."

It was one of the most difficult nights we'd had since becoming parents. And that says something in this house. I had not been that uncomfortable in a long time. I'd spent years learning how to accept the circumstances of my family. I'd continually readjusted my comfort levels to confront the newest issue I didn't even know I would ever have to prepare for. Just when I'd thought I had a handle on it, it was time to adjust again.

When Zac and I calmed down, we discussed our concerns with the director. I tried to explain that Jordan was in a position without support. In this public venue, she was stealing so much attention from other students and it was evident they were getting upset by her behavior. No matter what happened, they continued to let her flail. At no time did anyone step in and support her in any of the ways we had practiced.

The director responded that they loved working with Jordan and only saw her joy. They did not understand my concerns.

I pushed forward. Jordan does not have a lot of friends at school. She is a very social kid, but she is isolated in her program. Experiences like this further isolate her from her peers. We watched how few children congratulated her after the show. We saw them move their bags to avoid her company. We are teachers; we know how to read the body language of the kid who is an outcast. We wanted her to be more than just the girl on the playground other people were instructed to be nice to. She was more than just the kid who was treated with polite invisibility. She was an incredible kid and would make an even better friend.

Every child deserves to have success in whatever situation they are involved in. Success looks different for every individual child. Having an adult gently redirect her when she burst through a curtain would not have been embarrassing for her; it would have given her an opportunity to be treated with dignity.

The teacher expressed that they hadn't seen it that way. They just wanted her to have fun expressing her true nature. They wanted her to have an opportunity to be independent. They didn't want to dampen her star quality or draw even more attention to her.

"Ironically, more attention was drawn to her without your support. We are proud of her, but it was incredibly difficult for us to watch."

"We will take your concerns under advisement."

Change is slow-moving. There will forever be two versions of that night. It is the difference between how she sees the world and how the world sees her. They are both true. She ended the night with glory. I ended it with passion. It is only when we are faced with discomfort that we find the impetus for change.

Jordan and I were both ready to take on our next roles.

CHAPTER 63
Shakespeare, I'm Trying

Sophomore year of college at the University of Wisconsin–Madison, I signed up for Shakespeare 202 with a professor who was rumored to be one of the leading experts on the topic. Although I loved the writing, I didn't know if I actually understood it, so when she called on me for my interpretation of Edgar's lines in the final scene of *King Lear*—"Speak what we feel / Not what we ought to say"—I was a bit nervous. What could I possibly have to contribute?

I used what I knew. The concept of those lines resonated with me; it was something I wanted to aspire to, speaking what I felt. I relied on the "ought to" far more in my life than I was comfortable. I was afraid of making anyone more upset than they needed to be. I wasn't moving through my life lying, but I just wasn't always being honest with myself. This is one of the reasons I love literature; it invites each person to find their truth in the words. I used my personal frustration to empathize with Shakespeare's characters and shared my analysis, solely based on this one line. My voice filled the auditorium with what I was sure was some sort of rambling, but my professor simply stated, "Ask this girl if you have any questions about Shakespeare."

It was Shakespeare class; everything that was said verged on hyperbolic. However, it did confirm that while the language of this playwright made me incredibly nervous, I could still be good at it. It was a good lesson to learn. Even when we feel unsteady, we can surprise ourselves. I thought it was time to move on to other topics that made me nervous.

It was then I found my first therapist, a psychology major in the graduate school program. Her face grew red with each question and her hands were so sweaty, the pen slipped through them. I filled the air discussing the recent death of my maternal grandfather, and how I supposed I refrained from saying what I really thought because I might never see that person again. So I ended every conversation with a perfect little bow. This seemed like a good solution for me. That's the problem with being a person who analyzes words; you are too often analyzing your own. I don't know if this thesis was in fact true, because I stopped going to see that nice, nervous woman. I spent most of my sessions affirming for her that she was doing a great job, and ironically not talking about how I really felt at all.

It was over a decade before I sought the support of a therapist again. My entire identity had shifted, and everything I had been studying for had altered. Being a special needs parent became my first identity marker and was slowly erasing all the others. I was having a hard time reconciling the person I used to be with the person I needed to become. My solution was to say what I thought other people wanted to hear ("We got this, thank you") and avoid what I should have really said ("We need help") to them, and, most importantly, to myself.

When I was a child, I would only express stress through my dreams. During the day, I was a ball of energy and pep; however, at night, the anxiety would creep in. Sometimes my stress presented in a harrowing dream where I was desperately searching for a birthday cake or there was a dragon who would try to eat my dad. This pattern was reemerging as a special needs mom. If I could just make it to my bed at night, it would mean I would have a temporary lull from the onslaught of decisions, but lying down made it worse. The quiet mocked me with a false sense of relief. The dragon had turned its attention to devour me.

I tried therapy.

"Do you think there is something connected to your childhood that makes you unable to say how you feel about having a special needs child?" the therapist probed.

"I had a happy childhood."

I watched her hand slowly write, *unremarkable childhood*. She looked up at me. "I have all this space. There is nothing more to add here?"

There's that word again, "unremarkable." I felt like I'd disappointed her.

I'm sure I could have thought of something more to add. I considered my options. I had killed my sister's goldfish, Dotty, because it did not have a predilection for taking walks. I had always wanted a lead in the high school musical. And there was that boy I'd had a crush on for a decade—

She interrupted my thoughts. "I know someone who institutionalized their child with special needs."

"No, thank you. That is not what I had in mind."

"Well," she paused, "have you considered putting lavender under your pillow?"

I stopped going.

I tried again a few years later. This time with Zac. "We are looking for some advice about how to carve out time for ourselves while raising a child with special needs," we told her.

She listened to our story and smiled, as if she had the answer. Finally: the anecdote to finally be able to process everything that was swimming in my head.

"There is a keyword that will help you connect with your child."

Not a great start. We needed to talk about us, not Jordan.

"The concept is"—she leaned forward—"empathy."

We stopped going and I stopped looking.

I didn't need therapy. I had the strongest support system anyone could ask for: friends and family who loved me with an unending supply of time to hear me out. I thought I was emptying my tank, talking about my fears, frustrations, and concerns. However, as I grew more and more overwhelmed, the prescribed script stopped working. This was more problematic: I was saying what I ought to, but convincing myself it was the truth.

Enter therapist number four.

I found myself in one of the typical patterns that someone who didn't want to revisit pain uses: automatic pilot. If I discussed my struggles with general statements, I could skate over the issues that were hard to address. It would sound like this: *I have a child with a rare diagnosis. I thought my son needed brain surgery and his twin had cancer. Since my daughter was born ten years ago, my husband lost his mother and sister and I buried my grandfather, uncle, and cousin. We are tired.*

It's all true, but it is nowhere close to "speaking what I feel." In fact, writing summary sentences like that is the biggest clue that there is more to unlock. It is usually the hardest part of the process.

The new therapist advised me to sit in what is uncomfortable. Rather than deflecting it, distracting myself, or, my new hobby—eating it—I just needed to sit in it. Notice it. Own it. Release it.

I took this direction and applied it to everything except my life at home. I was eager to talk about the issues I wanted to focus on at work, for example. While we did address them, she continued to teach me that it is usually the spaces in our life where we feel the most secure that we can ask for help, because we can acknowledge what we need. It is the places where we never ask for help that usually point to the spaces where we feel the most vulnerable.

Of course, the English teacher in me loved this insight. "I am never afraid to ask for help at work, because I feel confident there. I don't often ask for help at home because I should be able to figure it out." And like any person who has spent years swallowing feelings, I literally blinked away some tears, made a joke, and changed topics—without even realizing it. Deflection is a powerful tool.

My therapist leaned forward in her chair and told me we needed to talk about something. "Leah, I'm not sure you have come to terms with your daughter's diagnosis."

I took a deep breath. "Well, I just wrote an entire book about how I did."

This made us both laugh.

"There's always room for another chapter," she suggested.

It gave me permission to offer myself a bit of a release, and to perhaps get a little closer to speaking what we feel when we speak the truth.

I am raising a child in a life that I did not anticipate. Her life is joyful. I feel selfish when I want to take a break from it, and I'm too afraid to ask for help. I am fearful about the safety of all my children, so I avoid relishing the calm because I am uncertain how long it will last. I am not sure I can recreate the happy childhood I had for my own children. I am lucky. I am lonely. I feel the responsibility to carry on the legacy of family members who are no longer alive. I am burdened by a self-imposed responsibility: if I can shoulder someone else's pain, then I can prevent them from any of the anguish I have faced. I spend too much time looking for truth in what should be fleeting thoughts.

Dear reader, it took me over seven years to write my truth. I invite you to sit in what is uncomfortable to find your own.

CHAPTER 64
I See You

To the woman in the doctor's office, I want you to know that I saw you. You also had a minivan-sized stroller. Your diaper bag was clean; I could tell because the piping was still pure white. I recognized that shirt, a snug-fitting royal-blue cotton with a built-in cardigan to create the perfect balance of comfort and presentability. You were missing your socks and had thrown on your gym shoes, a combination you wouldn't have been caught dead in three weeks ago, but today it's the furthest detail from your mind. I have been where you stand: a new mother in this doctor's office.

You smiled toward us. A genuinely warm smile.

The first time I walked into this office, my daughter was not much older than your son is now. Despite hearing this was the best geneticist in Westchester county, I didn't want to be here either. This is not a routine stop on the introductory tour of parenthood.

You took your son out of the stroller. He was still the age when he remained in a ball despite having space to stretch out. I love that stage. I saw you had wrapped his wristband from the hospital around the handlebar of the stroller. It is not the standard matching one you and your newborn receive on the birth date, but rather the one they give you when the child has been admitted to the surgical floor. We have three of them.

You sat next to us.

I smiled. You smiled.

I opened my mouth to say something. *Hi. I think I can relate to what you are going through. You are going to be okay. He's beautiful. Welcome to the club. You are doing great.* Would you have wanted me to acknowledge you? Would I have wanted someone to talk to me?

Instead, it was not my voice I heard.

"Look, Mommy. A baby. Hi, baby. When is your birthday? I have the same skin on my arm that I had when I was a baby. Look." Jordan thrust her face into our new companion's. "Were you born during Obama? I was."

You brushed away a piece of your I-haven't-been-able-to-dye-this-for-months hair and I gently translated. My motherly magic allowed me to understand every word perfectly. "She likes your baby and wants to know when he was born."

Your smile brightened. "Just a month ago."

I opened my mouth to say something again. *This is a great doctor. We started here seven years ago. Do you need anything? Do you have a support system?*

The nurse called, "Jordan."

You moved your legs out of the way so Jordan wouldn't trip over them. "Yes! Let the party begin!" she yelled. "See you later, baby!" Jordan blew a kiss in his direction.

I gathered our belongings and ran after my sprinting child. I turned around and caught you glancing down at your precious bundle. You looked up and met my eye.

I opened my mouth to say something. *I was where you were once. I was terrified. I didn't know how I would do this. Somehow, I am doing it. Look at how happy my daughter is.*

Instead, I smiled.

You smiled.

I never said anything, but I hope you heard every word.

CHAPTER 65
Challenger League

It's a crisp Sunday morning, and Jordan pops out of bed.

"It's soccer time!" she cheers.

She does not love anything about the actual sport. In fact, the last time she was in front of the goal, as the ball approached her, she stepped aside, let it pass, and then did a celebratory dance for the other team. She is cheering for the parts of the game she likes: seeing her crush (we will call him "Boy Brian"), her new bestie Mariella, and chatting with her soccer buddy.

Jordan is on a challenger league soccer team. It was started by two dads in our community who are athletes and coaches, and both have sons with special needs. The league pairs each player with an older neurotypical buddy who will help them to participate in the sport. It is everything Zac and I were looking for: exercise for Jordan, opportunities to be social, and a community to belong to.

She rushes to change out of her pajamas and gets dressed independently. Usually, it takes her about ten minutes to figure out which way to turn her shirt, but she is standing before me with an entire outfit appropriate for soccer, including two layers. She proudly shows me her fluffy, pink sweatshirt that reads *Be Kind*, and she puts her beloved Doc McStuffins hat on her head. "Let's go, Mama. Time to see my boyfriend." She says it with all the effort of speech therapy and the sassiness of a girl twice her age.

I think I need to take some ownership for the boy-craziness of this nine-year-old girl. When I was her age, I thought if you had a crush on a boy, it meant he was your boyfriend. I learned this was not the case when I bragged to my sister about my seven boyfriends in second grade. Jordan has stuck to the same adorable crush for the past four years. She has not spoken to him for two of those years, but her love is pure.

We arrive at the field. She shouts hello to him in the opposite direction so that he can't hear her, and then she runs straight into the loving arms of her most favorite human. Her new BFF, Mariella.

"We're sisters!" she shouts as she envelopes Mariella's body. "I like your hair today, Mariella. It is very fashionable."

Not only does Mariella understand everything Jordan says, she encourages her to say more. In class, she helps Jordan to wait her turn and answer a question when their teacher asks. On the playground, they escape into imaginary worlds as they giggle going down the slide. When they play Jordan's favorite game, "Who knows me best?", Mariella writes the name of Jordan's favorite Disney princess. Jordan knows Mariella likes the color red, and Mariella doesn't care that Jordan can't spell or write the word "red."

Their friendship began during speech therapy. Their shared connection over wigs made them arrange their own playdate for one Tuesday after school so they could continue "being fashionable." Nothing brings me more joy than to sit back and watch Jordan and Mariella in their matching rainbow bathing suits, trying on wigs, giggling at their own reflections, and modeling their matching friendship bracelets.

It feels as if the universe handed us the most wonderful Mariella-sized present. "Come on, Jordan," Mariella redirects her. "Let's play soccer."

Jordan walks toward the field to meet her new buddy for the day, a high school sophomore with long, brown curls. Her face lights up when Jordan approaches her. "Hi, I like your shirt."

"This is Jordan," Mariella says. "She loves coming to soccer. Mostly because she wants to talk."

"Sounds perfect. Nice to meet you, Jordan. Let's go play."

As I see the two of them walk away, I can tell from Jordan's body language that she is talking up a storm. She has learned to rely on her physical movements and gestures to help people understand her. I am sure the girl will get only a handful of what she says, but it is clear she is listening intently to every word. I didn't realize the coach had previously interviewed the buddies to see which one had the most knowledge about Jordan's favorite topic, *Descendants*. I can make out a bit of their conversation as I take my seat on the sideline.

"That is my crush boy, Brian. That is my BFF, Mariella. What are you going to be for Halloween? Who was the president when you were born? Do you know Mal's dad?"

When I thank the coaches at the end of the hour, I hope they know it is for more than just the game.

CHAPTER 66
Say Yes to the Dress

"If I am going to be like *Tuck Everlasting*," I said to my fifth-grade teacher, "then everyone else I know has to be like him too."

This announcement was out of turn, perhaps, but important. I planned on living forever and also taking everyone I loved with me.

This is one of my first memories of a genuine love story, a girl needing to choose whether to continue living her own life or give it up to be with the immortal boy she loved. It felt very plausible at age ten. My profound theory at this age was that finding a partner was like standing in line, waiting for lunch. If every other person just turned around and loved whoever was behind them, then everyone would be happy. Simple enough. This idealistic phase extended a few decades. I was the teenager desperately listening to the radio host Delilah and her love song recommendations, and dancing to Brandy's version of *Cinderella*. My high school yearbook predicted my future: *to marry a hopelessly romantic man and raise our chubby babies together*. And that was the revised version.

There must be part of the idealistic hopeless-romantic concept that is hereditary, because Jordan caught it. She is crazed by love, romance, and, most of all, weddings. Even before she had the language for weddings, she informed us of her sentimentality through television.

While her peers were watching *Mickey Mouse Clubhouse* and *Peppa Pig*, we were snuggled nightly watching *Say Yes to the Dress*.

This reality-based television show capturing brides on their search for their wedding dress had several repercussions. First, Jordan began to parrot the language she heard on the show, which means "sexpot" briefly worked its way into her repertoire. It also meant that every time we visited Costco, we had to search for Pnina Tornai–like ball gowns, which was how we discovered her panache for pink and puffy. When she picked out her outfits in the morning, we had to give her enough time to select three options, show them to her committee of stuffed animals, and then await her definite decision of saying "yes" to the dress. Her dedication to the show was so emphatic, my friend even wrote a letter to see if she could be a guest; we still have our fingers crossed they will respond.

In the middle of watching her favorite episode, the one where the dogs get married, Jordan turned to me and said, "I want a ball gown when I marry Daddy someday."

"Of course. That would be beautiful."

I loved that in Jordan's world, her dream wedding was with her father. This was very natural for little girls her age. It would explain all the kissing she tried to get away with. I couldn't help but let my mind wander to the "someday" she spoke of. *Will Jordan get married? Will she find someone to love? Will they love her back?*

Perhaps this is a question many parents wonder about their own child—what will his or her romantic future look like?—but in this case, it was difficult to think about. We had our parenting philosophy: have realistic expectations for what was possible, but maintain a sense of hope while looking ahead. Just because the diagnosis said *can't*, didn't mean she *couldn't*.

Nine years ago, we were wondering if she would walk or talk; now we are hoping for read and write. Would this mean one day we would consider a job? Living independently? Will she be able to navigate her way safely in the world?

The unknown has a way of spiraling. Will I be around to see her future? What will happen when Zac and I are no longer here? Who will take care of her? What will Jordan's adult years look like?

I don't know.

And for me—the young girl lost in fairy tales, love stories, and the concept of happily ever after—as it turns out, the story isn't that simple after all.

There is something more powerful. In the middle of a real life, an incredible love story unfolds. Talking with your child who was never supposed to speak. Spending the day running through the park with your children, and although they are at different speeds, they are running together. Eating dinner with your children, vibrant and healthy, despite the odds. Pushing past the boundaries to just be a family. Breathing in the simplicity of the day, when the world wants you to move so much faster.

And as for the future—well, I'll let you know.

Acknowledgments

In 1957, my grandfather, Julius Soled, published Fasteners Handbook, 415 pages of descriptions and diagrams about reference materials for engineers. In his acknowledgments, he thanked my grandmother for her secretarial skills and my mom and aunt for their patience while the book was "aborning." I had never heard this word before, a description of something coming into being, but it is the exact word I need to describe the process of writing a book and adding another story to our family legacy.

Because this story is all about legacy. It is a way to continue the stories of my family for my children. It is an opportunity to reframe how families with disabilities are seen. It is a giant hug of gratitude to the people along the way. Here's to you, the people who not only helped me to write this story but also celebrated our family odyssey during the past ten years.

This story would not exist without the incredible care of more than fifty doctors, receptionists, therapists, and teachers who have been with us from the very beginning. There will never be enough words (or construction paper cards) to express our gratitude for everything you do to keep every member of this family safe and moving forward. Your care does not stop with our children. You remind Zac and me every day that we do not have to do any of this alone. Thank you to Stefani, Regina, Rita, and Jackie for coming into our house of loving chaos. It is because of you I was able to move from just understanding Jordan's diagnosis to becoming an advocate for her.

To the families of the 5p- Society, your organization was our first phone call on the day of our diagnosis. You have been with us through every step (and you will be hearing from us when puberty hits!).

Thank you to the readers of the Loving You Big blog who bravely shared their stories with me and reminded me just how resilient special needs families are. You gave me the community I needed to continue writing to make a change.

To Laurie Scheer with the University of Wisconsin Writing Institute, thank you for listening to a handful of stories from a tired mom, seeing the potential for something more, and responding quickly to my excited emails.

To the brave writers at the When Words Count Retreat, thanks for listening to early drafts with empathetic ears.

Thank you to Nicola Kraus for the sage advice to help me find the vulnerability the book needed.

Thank you to the skillful minds of Noa Wheeler and Kaitlin Severini, who not only painstakingly read through each draft, but also quelled my first-time writer nerves.

To Jennifer Frank, thank you for your unwavering belief in me and what is possible. Your expertise, empathy, and friendship have pushed me to be a better writer.

To the incredible team at Warren Publishing for allowing my story to have a voice, your professionalism, enthusiasm and expertise have made this a rewarding experience.

For the incredible people in my corner, filling my life with support, and networking skills. Thank you to Tiffany Harris and everyone at Inclusion Matters by Shane's Inspiration for your mentorship and support of my mission. Thank you to Barbara Deutsch, Susie Orman Schnall, and the entire team at Nardi Media.

Thank you for the artistic eye and expertise of Linda Spock, Asha Hossain, Emily Dombroff, Sam Lembeck, Sarah Palefsky, and Norman Lavintman.

To the incredible network of families and loved ones that watched me and Rachel grow up: if you know what the Marx Brothers' room looks like, this one's for you.

To the neighbors and friends we have the pleasure of sharing our lives with, thank you for reading drafts of this book and always modeling empathy and kindness for our children.

As a teacher, you learn your strongest skills from observing the experts around you. To my own innovative teachers, forever captivating me with stories, thank you for inspiring my career. I am so grateful to the educators I have had the opportunity to work beside for the past fifteen years. You are doing the hard and important work.

To my wonderful students, you inspire me with your bravery to tell your stories. This is one book you don't have to annotate. I promise— there won't be any Post-it sticky note checks tomorrow.

To Lisa and Barbara, words will never do our gratitude justice. I wish I could bottle some of your calm and loving magic.

To those of you who lift me up, even when my voice shakes. Thank you Cathy, Katie, Nikole, Chandana, Allison, and Karen for inspiring my advocacy and opening your hearts to my family.

Thank you to the greatest support system Zac and I could ever wish for: Sam, Aliza, Alex, Scott, Melanie, Ben, Lara, Mandy, and Daryl. Without you and your families, Zac would have a lot of brisket to eat, and I would be locked in a bathroom somewhere, hiding in my oversized sweatpants and 5p- sweatshirt. We are the luckiest.

To the women who have always been listening: Alana, Julia, Michelle, Amy, Bryn, Seren, Diana, Rita, Lesley, and Natalie. You know what you mean to me. Thank you for the past twenty years of catching my brain and holding my heart.

This story begins with our families. Thank you, Jacquie and Amanda, for leaving behind a legacy of love. To my incredible in-laws, Phil and Debby: Thank you for welcoming me and our glitter-filled children into your loving home. You are the solid ground we need to keep our footing.

To my loving family: I think all those Thanksgiving plays we created shaped my storytelling. I love you all so much and am so grateful for your endless encouragement.

To Aunt Judy, my personal marketing maven, thank you for reading every word, and for validating and hugging this story into life.

To Rachel, from the moment you first held my tiny arms safely behind me so I wouldn't break anything in any fancy store, you have always been my safest place to land. To you and Brian: You show up for us in ways I didn't even know existed. Thank you for the unconditional love, hot sauce, and three perfect curly-haired nieces.

To my parents, Mona and Lenny. Thank you for teaching me what a great love story looks like.

To my children, Jordan, Austin, and Oliver: Thank you for letting me tell our story to help other people with theirs. If you read this one day, you did an excellent job sharing your mama with a computer screen for a few years. Thank you for your help in writing it while sitting on my head and knowing when it was time to celebrate with a gigantic dance party. You are my greatest joys. I love you big.

And to you, my Zachary: Fifteen years ago, I made a wish in that pond in Austin, Texas. Because of you, every day it comes true.

Bibliography

Bishop, Rudine Sims. "Mirrors, Windows, and Sliding Glass Doors." *Perspectives: Choosing and Using Books for the Classroom* 6, no. 3 (Summer 1990).

"Discrimination: Disabled People and the Media." *Contact,* no. 70 (Winter 1991): 45–48.

Mitchell, David T., and Sharon L. Snyder. *Narrative Prosthesis: Disability and the Dependencies of Discourse.* Ann Arbor, MI: University of Michigan Press, 2000.

CPSIA information can be obtained
at www.ICGtesting.com
Printed in the USA
BVHW051957290622
640924BV00002B/173